A SECOND EARTH

OTHER WORKS BY HAROLD ENRICO

Now, A Thousand Years From Now (Sono Nis, 1975)
Rip Current (Sono Nis, 1986)
Dog Star (Cacanadadada, 1990)

A
Second
Earth

Selected & New Poems

by

Harold Enrico

Edition and Afterword by

Ronald B. Hatch

RONSDALE PRESS
1997

A SECOND EARTH
Copyright © 1997 Harold Enrico

RONSDALE PRESS
3350 West 21st Avenue
Vancouver, B.C. Canada
V6S 1G7

Set in New Baskerville 11 on 13-1/2
Typesetting: Julie Cochrane, Vancouver, BC
Printing: Hignell Printing, Winnipeg, Manitoba
Cover Design: Ewa Pluciennik

Ronsdale Press wishes to thank the Canada Council for the Arts, the Department
of Heritage, and the British Columbia Cultural Services Branch for their support
of Ronsdale's publishing program.

CANADIAN CATALOGUING IN PUBLICATION DATA
Enrico, Harold, 1921–
   A second earth

   ISBN 0-921870-53-1

   I. Hatch, Ronald B.   II. Title
PS3555.N74S42 1997   811'.54   C97-910417-3

for
TERRY

Voi, che per li occhi passaste al core
e destaste la mente che dormia . . .

— GUIDO CAVALCANTI

ACKNOWLEDGEMENTS

Harold Enrico's poetry, translations, and essays have appeared in the following periodicals:

Poetry (Chicago), *Botteghe Oscure, The Nation, Prism international, Contemporary Literature in Translation, Books Abroad, The New York Herald Tribune, Commonweal, Madrona, Commentary, Mirror Northwest, The Christian Century, Sparrow, Proceedings of the Pacific Northwest Conference on Foreign Languages, Modern Language Quarterly, Italian-Americana, Other Than Review, Pacific Quarterly, Moana, West Coast Review, Saggi di Umanismo Cristiano-Pavia, Boletin — Piemontesi nel Mondo of Northern California,* and in the anthology, *A Garland for Dylan Thomas* (ed. George J. Firmage).

The poems from *Now, A Thousand Years From Now* (1975) and *Rip Current* (1986) are reprinted with the kind permission of Sono Nis Press.

C'est vrai; c'est à l'Eden que je songeais!

— Arthur Rimbaud,
UNE SAISON EN ENFER

CONTENTS

from
RIP CURRENT

from

NOW, A THOUSAND YEARS

FROM NOW

I TRY TO REMEMBER

for Olive

I try to remember where I have been.
A dead snake loved this dust.
A she-hawk hovered over that nest.
The sun crashed down behind that hill.

I heard the wind's harps
In the same trees,
Scraped through similar weeds
Over different stones.

Thunder shook the mountain tops.
Old grandfather of our dead tribe,
How he barked!

Like a flint knife slitting a deer hide,
Lightning slashed the sky.

In the fossil darkness
Among my mother's bones,
Listening to the lapping voices
Of her blood
In her fern-branching veins,

Rocked in her roots,
I crouch between the pathway
And the human heart.

INDIAN SONG

I was born on a river
With a slow voice
In a country
Of lichen and rock.

The bird-tracked hand
Of a woman
Laid me on the ground
On the top of a hill.

I watched the lynx,
Listened to the locust,
Waited for the hawk
To talk to me,

While the sun howled
In his yellow skin
And the wind sniffed my shadow
On the hill.

THE FLEECE OF THE RAM

美 MEI: beautiful; a big sheep; also
abbreviation for Ya-*mei*-li-cha, America.

I / THE ROOT*

1

Suppose the key word to be *antipode*. . .
the river grips the virgin rock.

"The person who contracted to build my boat
engaged to have it in readiness by the 20th inst. . . .

set out at 4 o'clock p.m.
under a gentle breeze . . .
a succession of grasses, trees,
marshes teeming with birds . . .
currents strong with riffles,
oars hard to use . . ."

A dove flew safely through clashing rocks,
The kingfisher hovered over white water,
scolding us, many small birds
as thick as insects, twittering in sedge.

* Quotations (in original spelling) are from the journals
  of the Lewis and Clark expedition and from
  Thomas Jefferson's instructions to the explorers.

*

"And this medesene man could foretell things . . .
that he had told of our coming into their country,"
and they thought us gods dropped among them:
helmsman, navigator, peacemaker of tribes . . .

"These natives have the Strangess language,
but I found them much pleased at the Danceing of our men,
the women passionate, fond of caressing . . .
Danceing, giving away their bracelets."

— She was so beautiful that when she slipped into the tent
the storyteller could not tell his story . . .
"The old squaw, half blind, crouching in a corner
had lived more than a 100 winters,
& when she spoke, great attention paid to what she said"

>The roots of the rock outlive the crown.
>And *my boy Pomp* had his monument.

2

Among your Instruments and Apparatus,
you will find one set of Gold Scales*

"to weigh the industry of tribes,
their language, traditions, monuments,
the extent and limits of their possessions.

Is suicide common among them?
— I have done the business.
My good Servant, give me some water.
— He had shot himself in the head with one pistol
& a little below the breast with the other."

The wind grapples open grasses, rocks, trees

in those "scenes in which you were engaged
with the promise of a city
at the confluence of rivers . . .
or a place near Sea or River
resembling the situation of Alexandria
with respect to the Nile . . ."

" — A root they have, efficacious remedy
in cases of the bite of a Rattlesnake . . .
To this I have added the horns of an animal
called by the natives the Mountain Ram . . ."

Under his hair he is clothed with a very long fur,
    shines golden
        in the sun.

* Thomas Jefferson's instructions to the explorers

1

The moon pulls great waters.
How articulate the wind is in the leaves,
But it does not want to tell me who I am.
I think I am somewhere between sleep and a stone.
I ask the sun where I have been.
My father mowing grass does not know.
My mother does not want to say.
I taste weeds to understand what a bird sings.
I am an Indian all day
Under the plum tree in the backyard.
An old blanket pinned to grape laths
Is my tepee. I am Chief Bear Skin,
Last of the Yakimas to smell free wind.
The wind cannot tell the distance
Between 1827 and 1927,
Nor can I.

2

A photograph, inked too black, in the newspaper,
Of three Yakimas,
Wears the same scowl. Pennsylvania Avenue in 1901,
Stumps down the middle, watch-fobbed Saxons in front of the
                                                                        hotel,
Was what my mother saw.

You look like an Indian! You look like an Indian!
My mother's black Italian hair,
Tossed over her forehead, dries in the sun
On the back porch.

"Ka-e-mox-nith was so beautiful
That when she stepped into the tent
The old men stopped talking." When she left,
Their voices were like the dry scraping of insects
In the yellow pines.

3

Old and sick, Wah Kukhiah rode up the Yakima Valley
With his daughter to the forest.
At the foot of the mountains
He told her to go home and rode on alone.
In the half-darkness at the edge of a scree,
In a dazzle of light, a stranger sat
On a boulder, looking at him:
"Do not be afraid. Close your eyes,
And you will see."

4

The plum tree in the sunlight
Sways in the last warm wind,
Branch dancing with branch.
With a bow bent from a willow switch,
I shoot an arrow straight across the garden
Into a bed of hollyhocks.

I got him! My tribe will not go hungry.
I know who I am!

Kamiakin: the Last Hero of the Yakimas by A.J. Splawn and
Drummers and Dreamers by Click Relander

My forehead bows to the sound of water,
    faint through trees.
A warbler in the lilac answers
    a warbler in the pine.
May spills over, fluent with leaves,
    redundant in the mirror of the pond.
Happy in weeds, I dawdle through trout lilies,
    gold on the hillside,
      nibbled over by cows and butterflies.

        Stooping over corollas
        I own their nuggeted anthers,
        and break stem after stem
        to bleed against my palm.

Wild with the incense of cottonwoods,
by the hobo dump, wreathed with early smoke,
the river curls, ice in the town's arms,
sleepy with salesmen and women,
haggled out of dreams,
money under every pillow,
under every hill,
wise with the intercourse
of vaginal mines.
        In the schoolroom's chalked silence,
        I perspire, stranger to the fists
        scrawling virgin paper with accusing consonants.

IV / THE CEMETERY

Love your mother's face
bowed over blossoms,
her hands arranging them
for your grandfather's grave.

In the front yard,
two bushes of lilacs,
tall as the house,
one white and one violet,
bloom every year
for Decoration Day . . .
     Walt Whitman dead for thirty-seven years,
     the Civil War over for sixty-four,
     the olive-backed thrush or the hermit
     singing in the canyons around the town.
Your grandfather, for whom
Victor Emmanuel meant more than Lincoln,
wrote from the Shoshone to his dying mother in Italy:
Don't despair of Death.
È una Gran Bella Cosa.

"You'll never make Americans
of these goddam wops,"
the foreman said.

In the cemetery,
a Mediterranean bay of blossoms,
white and violet in coffee-can urns,
billows against the stones.

V / TO CESARE PAVESE

Cesare Pavese, Death had your eyes,
not the eyes of an American starlet,
blue, blank.

The road, green, transparent,
shaded by alder trees,
emerges at the gate of Sovana.

The wind whines in the canebrake,
hisses in the vineyard,
and you weren't afraid . . .

the little viper of Italy
so much more venomous
than the American rattlesnake.

Picture Rome in the Rockies,
hollyhocks against a gray board fence.
"Hemingway, did you ever see
the green hills of Piemonte?"

"So many countries, so many portents."
And your extreme equation:
"Stoicism is suicide."

"Americans are not realists."
Imagine *Moby Dick* in Italian,
Captain Ahab, his eyes,
fierce blue.

Your sea is wine-dark,
the hawk hovering at its edge.
The root of fire
grips the ultimate rock.

VI / THE COAL MINE

Don't bullshit me, Mr. Lawrence!
How shall we recognize our own fathers
    "in caos converso,"
their palms bleeding in the fossil damp
while the Johnny Bull boss roars at the end
of the tunnel in the Eocene dark,
and the carbidian flames in the middle of their foreheads
pitch pantomimes of shadows
on the ultimate wall?
How shall we tell the flesh from the shade it throws?
"Tu credi che qui sia il Duca d'Atene?"

Quotations from Dante's "Inferno."

VII / THE RAM

In sheep-grass weather, clear bells found me.
I climbed to hear them while I slept.
Sheep grazed the hill above our house.
I heard them nibbling in my sleep.
Jangling bushes tossed on my pillow.
The walls baaed with the browsing flock,
Yapped with the fox-tailed dogs. I ran toward
Morning, blue above my father's gate.

A dry breeze rattled the dusty pines.
Pack horses, nudging luminous grasses,
Flicked their tails after flies. My ears followed
The oaths of Spanish herders.
I raced the hill slope after the easy flock,
Slipped, quick as a lizard, under barbed-wire,
Whipped across an acre through a cloud
Of pollen, gold upon my arms;

Waded through briars, tangling my hips
A thistle snapped at my thigh. I cleared
A meadow, over the mine of a mole,
Past a lark, warbling to weeds.
A pigeon tilted equal wings
Against the light I made. Wide-awake,
I leaped over the dreaming flock and sank
My fists into the fleece of the ram.

BUT LUCIFER, HE FELL

There was a wish that stanched a flood:
An angel's sidelong whisper to a dove.
The animals had shuffled off into the wood.
Deep in the leaves, the squirrels made love.
The wind-eyed ark, stove on the rocks,
Sent old Noah sprawling in the mud.
His sea legs trembled, testing stones;
His eyes admired the surer fox.

But Lucifer, he fell all day among
The nightingales whistling beneath the stars,
And even now wages his brilliant wars.
His fall had saved him all his bones
With no one there to marvel that
An angel falls as neatly as a cat.

THE COAL MINE / 1931

1

There are many ways to sleep.

When I was ten, I slept
deep enough for roots,
far enough for a wind
from infinity to find me.
The wind's time was mine.
The cricket repeated at nightfall
what the katydid rasped
all afternoon on the pile of ties
by the railway siding.

I played under the arc light,
climbed home to the moon.
My mother's hair illuminated her bed.
My father's walk was dark and long
down the incline to the bituminous seams.

In the tangled underbrush,
the thrush sang and sang.

2

The next day,
the mole's domes
redeemed the yellow pines
from the heat at the headwaters
of the Yakima River,
defined what counts —
the coolness of roots.

3

Where I am, I dream.
A wind from the peaks
curls up in the hollyhocks.
The energy of a whole afternoon,
gathered in one trumpet flower,
bells back a fanfare to the sun.
The late light hangs, a hive from a branch.
A leaf is what the sky needs.
A spider strings a wire from rose to rose,
lies in ambush
like a lion at the edge of a veldt.
One father's as good as another —
earth's or Eden's —
watching the spider
pounce through light.

I cannot see the light.

4

I wait for the man-trip.
The dark takes me down.
My father kneels in the deepest mine.
I rummage through other tunnels,
explore wider entries
humming with different hoists.
Fossil leaves flicker across my palms.
I dig into old earth
above older rocks.

I hear buried streams
filling with silt.

5

Black is the color of my father's hands.
Black is for death.
My father is more than that.
I can see in the dark.

6

My veins carry my blood away
into the same dark
past his roots.

HE NEVER WISHED FOR WAR

In winter my father spoke American.
In summer Italian was for the leaves.
For him, grapevines looped over every backyard fence.
Leaf mold was always ready to take him
Where he cared. Love was where the roots were.
He never wished for war.

When goldenrods powdered the roadsides,
And balsam roots multiplied the sun,
His thumb favored the apple,
Tested the ripening plum.

He sold the Chev and planted pear trees
On the driveway. In time, fruit
Bent the boughs. On winter evenings,
Slicing d'Anjous with a penknife, he feasted,
Licked ambrosia from his dripping thumbs.

HOMECOMING

By memorized ranches, houses named by heart,
Barbed-wire fences wound the dreaming miles.
Colts nuzzle mares in tooth-sheared pastures;
Red barns, like hens, squat glad in dust.
Tires grind to a stop in gravel. Frogs declaim
American from ditches creamed with spawn.

Wind flaunts the scarecrow's sleeve, who grins
Away the garden, gloating over dandelions.
The sow snores in her dream of milk and corn.
Licked by a momentary sun, straws blaze
Upon the gateside muck. Calves bawl.
Light drowns the honeysuckle on the wall.

ANOTHER LOOK

We were sure we had been this way before
Beside the burnt fields of blackened stubble,
As we stopped the car by the vacant ranch
And walked to the house, looking in
On what we had already seen.

We could not say how we were sure,
Or how long we peered into the half-dark rooms.
A dog barked beyond blue smoke in the hollow,
Leaves burning at year's end.
A heron skimmed the low wind over a pond
By the poplars tumbling into yellow ruin.
Our pale reflections smiled back from the window glass.
Our arms brushed the dust on the window sills.

When had we counted the hours chiming in those rooms
And looked out where we were now looking in?
The moss had grown deeper on the north side of the roof.
Long ago, our heels had worn the linoleum thin.

Slowly, we walked back through the gate
Hanging askew on a cracked leather hinge.
Nor could we say when we drove away
That we would not return.

TU FU AFTER 1200 YEARS ON A VACANT RANCH IN THE WESTERN MOUNTAINS

Black apples. Broken branch.
Frost sparkling on scarp.
A painting of pine trees for a screen:
A grove for the old hermits of Mount Shang.
Rope of light lassoing a vacant ranch.
Leaves, keen as knife blades, falling.
Blue jay on pole. Red bull in yarrow.
Aureole around the sun. Regiments
Of thistles bannering a field.
Deer hide nailed onto barn door.
Mare skull on pile of stones.

Tu Fu's voice across 1200 years.
Somewhere, always a war.
Hair streaked with white on return home.
Wife's face swimming beyond tears.
Krak! Krak! heron at river's edge.
The fields of Tung-Kuan.
Blue smoke on horizon.
White bones tossed into nettles.

Based on a poem by Tu Fu (A.D. 713–770)

A SAME KIND OF LIGHT

I knew a good man once,
self-appointed caretaker of the town dump,
built himself a shack out of packing cases and car bodies
and crammed it with junk.
A week after he died, we found him,
his face chewed away by rats.

The elder bush blossomed at the edge of ashes.
He kept a sprig in a rusty can.
Starlings and sparrows swooped from hawk weed
to peck at bread crumbs in his hands.
Raccoons followed him around like puppies
under the spicy cottonwoods.
He taught a crow to pronounce God's name.

Abba! roared the thunder: Abba! again and again.
Rain slaked the thirst of the dandelions.
Abba! cried their gold to the good man and his friends.
Stripping to his skin, he stomped across the cinders,
waving an elder branch around his head, yahooing
in a light purer than the moon's.

A same kind of light crowned the weeds.

WALKING A LONG WAY
THROUGH WOODS

Walking a long way through woods to meet him,
Light signals his rooftop,
A star or moon sputtering through bare branches,
Laburnum or lilac scraping the eaves.

We slide the door bolt noiselessly,
Slip into the pitchblack room
Where he dozes in an easy chair,

Waiting for someone to call,
Friend, enemy, anyone

To lure into his corner
Under the dust
Drifting over everything.

THE GATES

Two eagles glide so slow, easy in air
Above the barn, they lull themselves to sleep.
I meet my brother's shadow where
The field is shorn to crumbling by his sheep.
We glare at each other between the grass root and the thorn,
The gate of ivory, the gate of horn.

The naked branches of the willow tear
The sky to shreds. I wear the dying sun.
He wears the hot wind in his hair
Among the beasts that crawl, the beasts that run.
My left hand weighs the shadow of his head
Between the gate of gold, the gate of lead.

Wound in my linen sheets last night,
I dreamed a lion striding down to drink,
His mane blazing with supernatural light
Beneath the moon, on the river brink,
Stared at me with our father's eyes
Between the gate of truth, the gate of lies.

ADORATION

for Terry

The eye in August lingers on the leaf
And thorn beneath the bronzen rose. Sun burns
Upon the bush and wall and warms the worm.
Cicadas grate the dusty heat,
Chirr in the air their dry insistent cries,
Shrill in the grasses where the tight seed cracks.

But ear imagines and the heart invents
Old fables of cold holly Christmases
In winter Hollands: skaters on a pond,
And brown smoke drifting from tall timbered houses
Around a cattle stable in a wood,
Glowing with light beyond the light of stars.

Heart dreams of adorations of dark kings
And northern shepherds, music of lyres and horns
Ringing through junipers and falling snow,
And angels caroling a straw-haired child
While ice blackens the vine that grips the stone.
The leaf of August burns to finer dust.

TWELFTH NIGHT

Daughters scatter crumbs for winter sparrows.
Sons lick plums beside the tell-tale hearth.
The lamb bleats in his humpbacked barn.
Diked with ice, the hill spring pours pure wine.
The garden owns twelve nights of snow, scrawled
With mice feet, signed by a sparrow's toes.
The mole's wide paws, like hands, fold in
A griefless sleep beneath the rose tree's roots.

At midnight, warm old wine with cinnamon.
Drink to the three men on their tired beasts.
Sing in the kitchen under golden gourds,
And feast on apples from the cellar crib.

The thirteenth morning, on the blinding snow,
Twelve sparrows dive on midnight's crumbs.

LOVE'S BURNING

Kneeling to kindle fire
    among cold bricks,
I fan flames to grapple
    a nest of sticks:

then feed log after log
    onto the famished grate,
as if summer's woodpile
    could ever satiate

a fire's rapid hunger
    on a wintry night,
oak branch or pine knot
    appease such appetite.

UNDER VIRGO

Sometimes in mid-September, she ponders
The cold configuration of the stars,
The ruling signs of her declining year:
The hills already burning with autumn,
Vine maples flickering like broken flames,
Frost in the lower mountains, snow
Above the timberline, red deer bedded down
Beneath the golden pines. The river froths
Against the rocks, the flicker calls
From fir to fence, and summer-like
September glows again while cottonwoods
Decay into silver dust.

What promise from the ghosted grotto of the dead
Will make her blood run warm again
In bronze October? What portent of resurrection will fall
With the bright leaves breaking from the bough?
Mist drifts across her morning meadow.
The partridge whirrs through the yellow larches.

LATE OCTOBER WALK

Mist slips into your pockets — insubstantial coin —
Having bribed the spruce trees, branch by branch,
Converting them beside the road
Into shivering ghosts haunting the autumn air.
The road ends at a gate, bought out by briars.
Thorns post the pasture. Restrain your eager hand
And drop the latch!   Fierce in the mist,
A crow announces what he owns.

A scarecrow, silly in his father's rags,
Leers you away from his golden corn.
That woman, raking leaves, turns into a witch
And cackles toothlessly as flames she sets
To autumn's litter crackle beneath her pot.
Go home, damp straggler, with your stick and dog!
The maple's crown is not for sale!

Hunch homeward to your chair beside the fire
To munch winesaps bought at market price,
Your pockets bulging with nothing but mist,
Meager loot! October hoards the rest,
Mother of dark ferments, patroness
Of compost, black manure of promised earth.

SEPTEMBER

Though the light of September shall discover
The golden leaf on the bough,
The bitter fruit and the mellow,
The yellow pear and the medlar;

Though silver above the shadow,
The wood-owl's feather shall hover
And fall in the dust that covers
The thimble skull of the sparrow,

Deep, deep in the ground, low, low,
The root still clutches and labors,
Down through loam, umber and shallow;
And though these loveless lovers

Lie in the shade of leaves grown yellow
In a wood where the echoes quaver,
The hound shall bay all day in the hollow,
The vixen fall, and the dark roots have her.

SOME LINES FROM DANTE'S
AL POCO GIORNO

I came
  to the dim daylight,
  to the great circle's shade
  on the road that ends at the boundary stone
  by the crevice among boulders —
          descent into Avernus
  the pathway into the earth's heart.
  There is none into yours.

When you wore a garland of grass in your hair,
you drove the thought of any other woman out of my mind
and mingled so many yellows and greens in the flowers
          in your hands,
that Love came to walk in the shade of high ferns and alders.

  At this moment, swans are whistling over the larches.
  Light melts on the shale of Quartz Mountain.
  The green of spruce is almost an icy blue . . .

I have seen you dressed in such deep green . . .
Now frozen like snow, you stand in the mountain's shade.
I would have slept my life out on a stone,
eaten bear grass to have walked in the shade of your arms.

          But you disappear
into the first patch of green below the timberline
like a stone rolling down among the commingled grasses.

ISLA DE DOLORES

An island (now Destruction Island) off the coast
of Washington State. Juan de la Bodega and
Bruno Heceta were the first Europeans to sight
it in 1775.

Suddenly, you loom out of the early fog
As we watch from under the mainland pines
And imagine ourselves arm in arm,
Stalking love where love cannot thrive
Among your salal-knotted graves,
While the beam from your lighthouse
Grapples the fog's vagrant wings,
And your rocks reckon more sorrows
Than Juan or Bruno dreamed,
Abandoning you to your desperate name.

How long shall we thrash among your enameled leaves,
Tracking down what we cannot find,
Not brave but resigned to your uneasy rains
And difficult gales, ignoring the giant slugs
That measure you grain by grain,
And the cormorant that explores you from the air?

Someday, you will slip into the ocean's fluent grave
And settle forever into sea-wrack and silt,
Your name a dissonance on the merest wind,
Whispered back by our lingering ghosts,
Arms around each other's waists, still possessed by the fury
That drove us across your easeless face
Under the walls of your sleepless tower,
Your signal of danger, your voices of sorrow.

THE COLD EDGE

You walk beside me by the sea's cold edge
Between sound and silence: voices that grow
From water, shriller voices of the gulls,
And our two voices that the wind has spared,
The pines repeating what the deepest sea
Has said, a far beginning and an end
Whispered like perilous music in your ear.

Beyond the sea's declivities, your ear,
Cupped toward the scoured promontory's edge
Beside the peeling logs at north-land's end
Has listened to the salt-tongued voices grow
And ricochet from wave to grave, from sea
Rock to winter wreckage patrolled by gulls
Contending for what the raven spared.

What lovers' voices have the waters spared?
Meanwhile, the deafened turnstone cocks his ear
Toward stillness at the ocean's core, noisier gulls
Explore the tideline's indented edge
For sweeter litter pitched like manna by a sea
Whose deep discanting will not end.
Rather those incantations sometimes grow

Into a voiceless sigh. So voices grow
Into a spray of stillness in a seaside garden spared
No trellises of roses at land's end,
Blossoms above a lintel or a grave. But ear
Against a conch, you listen to a purer sea
Beside a clearer coast of whiter gulls,
The faintest blathering of waters at the edge

Of bone, imaginary oceans at the edge
Of nothing, waves that whisper as they grow
Like grasses crowned with mist and gulls
Against a sea-wall that the gales have spared,
Unceasing cooing of the coolest sea,
Reiteration of a voice that does not end,
Soothing the channel of your dreaming ear,

As vague and sea-washed as the dolphin's ear,
A sea unrolling in a shell from edge to edge.
But even the jetty stones will crumble in the end,
Your tissues madden, you begin to grow
Into a pink anemone beneath the sea,
Deaf as a flower to the waves and gulls.
So finally your ear may not be spared.

Although these voices all have spared
The whale's tympanum and the osprey's ear,
The turnstone's and the hunting gulls'
Alert to more than what the wind growls at the edge
Of gravel. Down beneath another sea,
What distant voices, death's or love's, gather for an end
And in the mounting darkness grow

And grow, flooding the sharper grasses spared
No end in stillness? What woman's ear
Can survive the voices off that voiceless sea
Forsaken by the turnstone and the gulls,
As vacant as the sky beyond the landless edge?

THE GRAVES OF THE INDIAN WOMEN

1

Welling up out of invisible crevices among the boulders,
Secret holy places only your ghosts visit,
The dark seeps like your death blood across the ground.

The blind moon, oldest crone of your tribe,
Sinks down on her knees, groping for your bones
Scattered by grave robbers in the dying summer grass,
Her fingers fluttering from grassblade to grassblade
With the wind.

   Oh, you were beautiful!
   We pity your dead bodies.
   We pity the chiefs and braves who loved you.
   Their hands are leaves that will fly with the fall winds.

   Their mouths are mountain flowers in the high meadows,
   Bent and broken by early snow.
   In the low valleys, mullein and heal-all
   Smoulder to cinders in their arms.
   They wade knee-deep in your dust
   And in their own.

   Another summer corrodes Major Garnett's iron wrists
   And the wrists of his men who set fire to your tents
   And chased you and your children barefoot down
                                        the valley
   After they had cinched five of your braves to pine trees
   And crumpled them, five shots splintering the
                                        crystalline air,
   Leaving them for coyotes and crows . . .

Your ghosts drift away now with your chiefs and braves
And the stars and the full summer moon
Down the white gorge of eternity
With deer and elk, grizzly bears
And mountain goats running before you forever
Over loose stones and gray roots.

    2

But you always return
To haunt our own broken stones and dying roots.
In the late fall, if we listen closely
We can hear your ghost voices under the cottonwoods.

      One of your sorrels, long dead,
      Neighs by the stream edge.

    3

This morning, we finished stacking firewood
On the cabin porch against the mountain winter.
Two jays bickered all afternoon
In the sunlight in the bull pines.
The lake no longer reflects geese speeding south.
The mountains are weighed down with darkness.

    4

It is midnight.
The fire is almost out.
The cabin's one room is cold, and we blow out the candles.
Wrapped in our blankets not far from your bones,
We shiver at the first breath of snow from the east.

A cougar
   Padding across pine needles beside the door
      Barely ripples our first sleep.

      In our dreams tonight, and yours, behind walls
      And walls of snow piled upon snow,
      Now, a thousand years from now,
      The cougar pads across the dying coals.

THE BEAVER DAM

"L'espèce des castors serait très préférable."
—Voltaire, DICTIONNAIRE PHILOSOPHIQUE

The day after the president was shot,
My son and I climbed to the beaver dam
Beyond the hill crest in a logged-off hollow

Unkempt with slash and muddy water and sloshed along
The wheel-scarred road, gashed through a hemlock grove,
Fertile with toadstools, nurtured by hard rains,

Amanitas, sinister, perverse
With many deaths erupting through the musty humus,
Until we reached the pond's dark bulwarked water

Where clever sluices lapped an ancient stillness,
Snared by the snags between the squalid clouds
And littered earth. We marveled at the dam

And lodge the beavers had built, the alder trunks
Chiseled into stout logs, chinked with mud,
A watery farm for a contented family,

The dozing kits snuggling against the walls
Of their domed house, and marveled at that life,
Old as a fossil, like a diorama

Of a glacial age, anachronistic
Upon a complicated and human earth.
Nootka whalebones clouted slaves to death.

The lynched half-breed kicked Okanogan wind.
The *Tonquin* reddened green abundant harbors
With beaver blood. But chisel teeth cut clean,

The father's and the son's, by crystal ponds,
Although the steel-jawed rushes still betrayed
Them for the coinage stacked upon their pelts,

And stockade guns marched slaughter to their domes,
The tomahawk and blunt square-headed axes,
Black jewels in the mud . . . Turning, we thrashed

Our way through Devil's Club and iron briars
Back to the bull-dozed road above the town,
Its roofs already echoing with funeral drums.

DEAD FIELD MOUSE

Rigid on its back among the litter of fallen leaves,
Grazed by my boot, the dead field mouse flips over
To land on its belly, ready for running somewhere
Without going anywhere through the grass
That would have offered it
Safe conduct to wherever home was.

Between the crossed boughs of the alders,
Light slopes down to illuminate
Fur, tail, eyes, claws, and I think I see
It move, but it is only the wind
Shifting its body on the leaves.

Between apparition and recognition,
A dark wind whistles the truth.
My bones shudder in the sudden cold.
Tiberius in his palace stalks from room to room:
Lear's 'never' rings out five times from the cliff.
Home is where it never was.

FROM THE TOP OF QUARTZ MOUNTAIN ON THE TWENTY-FIFTH ANNIVERSARY OF KANDINSKY'S DEATH

From the top of Quartz Mountain:
deer, trees, the shapes of stones
— hexagonal crystal, unblemished agate —
the Great Perfection's precious emblems
out of the mountain's deepest heart.
The elk's great antlers brush the aspen leaves.

The light blows strong,
remembering to sing
over the black wave,
through the forked branch of the pine,
    (At Neuilly, Kandinsky,
    precise as a chemist,
    mixes his own colors,
    lifts the shade at one o'clock sharp,
    letting in the light.
    Between the necropolis and the Champs-Elysées
    the rainbow arches over the iron gate.
    In the center of each painting,
    zero is absolute in a timeless zone.)

On the top of Quartz Mountain
the sun shifts from spruce to pine,
and the late afternoon shadows
dapple the deer at the edge of the scree,
the golden plover in the grass by the western hemlocks —

when suddenly the sun explodes,
black begetting black at the edge of red.

Yama, how your blackness shines,
a black bird in a nest of stars!

GRIZZLY

The webbed toes of waterbirds padding
estuary mud kept me awake for hours last night,
although wild geese, lost in fog,
lifted me almost to the edge of dream:
unclouded larches, pure Canadian fords,
peaks that contrived to blend their colors
with the tatters of a dying sun.

Meanwhile, my heart-beat timed me
back to a sleepless earth,
but toward morning I climbed a high moraine
against a wind from the North
and slid down into a Yukon of faultless woods
where I hunted the Grizzly in a foot of snow
and tracked him down into a bog.
Waist-deep in water, I flailed my arms.
A flock of widgeons whistled over my head.
The sweet smell of the beast clung to my hair
and penetrated my skin through my dripping clothes.

> Furred, my hands stretched their claws
> and scratched at the early stars.
> I felt a blizzard blowing under my hide.
> Sleepily, I dragged myself to a pile of roots.

> In a nest of leaves
> I slept that winter out.

VERTIGO

Four hawks sweep the light with perfect wings
Above the canyon's farther lip. Deer drowse
In draws, and on a ridge two red mares browse
On meager blades. A katydid sings and sings
Its desiccated old lament upon
A mullein stalk. A thread of smoke, a mile
Away, climbs perpendicular a while,
Then veers west. A doe, shielding her fawn,
Clatters behind a bush as we drive past
Up to the bare bones of the Eocene,
Black fire-made rock broken with early green.

We stop and step out into the blast
Of unobstructed wind, clutch at the car
In vertigo before a sheer abyss.
No bird sweeps that air. Black rocks hiss
With all that wind. And we know where we are.

THE RIVER TATSUTA IN AUTUMN

Hokusai,
mad on drawing,
who had to show
the Shogun,
the son-of-a-gun,
that he could paint
as well as the next clown,
tore off the door
of the temple
and laying it on the floor,
slashed a wild river
across it in indigo;
and yanking a rooster
from a cage,
he dipped its feet
in a pot of red
and shooed it across
the river of blue.
"The river Tatsuta:
the end of autumn,"
he bowed.
And the Shogun, the bum:
"Hey, what a show!"

THE BLIND POET

A poet gone blind dreams he sees
The winter moon float out of the alders
And sail over field after field of snow.

All summer long, light leaping off of stone
Was light lost upon his face:
Early June's, as cool as evening rain.
The light of mid-August, tangled in goldenrods,
Burned more burnished than his figurative sun.

October spilled not light but smoke
Of smouldering leaves across his sleeve;
He tasted ashes, stumbled through dust,
Swallowed his own kind of fear.
Late light tightened around his face,
A golden mask on a frame of bone.

Now he sits motionless
Beside a window glassed
With northern nights, frosted by his breath,
Watching the moon sail over
The lost snow fields of his mind:
Pure light, pure metaphor.

THE DESERT AND AFTER:
LA TERRA PROMESSA

for Giuseppe Ungaretti

Over your desert and after —
the limitless sand —
a light like the sea's
interspersed with gulls and terns
suspended between two winds,
the wind from hereafter,
the wind from the land,
when the eye sees
and does not see
the sun descending
to the chasm's edge,

    equally displaying
    beach and bar,
    the living and the dead,
    where the river bleeds
    into the ocean's bed,

while between the wave that rises,
and the wave that falls,
the ship rides at anchor,
that brings you to us again,
over the horizon and beyond

in the light of a tide
that freezes anchor, keel, sails
into mortal signs
at the landless edge:

time for the wasp
to prepare her cell,
time for the hawk
to construct her nest,
time for the light of hereafter
to wash every stone
of your Promised Land.

Giacomo Leopardi,
you were aware, if anyone ever was,
of the obstacles facing translation
from tongue to tongue,
from heart to heart.
How sweetly a solitary finch
sings this holiday evening on the weathervane
on the barn while a thrush,
predicting rain, chants a darker song
in an alder swale,
not at Recanati but in Aberdeen, Washington.
We drown in infinite seas of light,
our bodies no longer ours.
The poem reads like a translation
from an extinct language,
illegible signs on the ashen pages
of the ageless heart.

BRANCHES

Near Lugano or at Borgeby Gård
(What does it matter if snow
obliterates a vineyard
or bends birch trees to the ground?)
Rilke, head bowed at his desk by the window,
ignores the falling snow.
The poem he is writing
grows like a squiggly black vine or tree
on a snow-blinding page,
vine shoot, pliant birch branch
trembling on an infinite wind.

      Zero catapults through his brain.
      He hunts out a metaphor in space.
      Frost grapples old roots:
      branches crackle in icy air.

      At home in the Okanogan, snow
      piles up for days against the cabin walls.
      Coyotes circle the winter camp.
      A bull elk starves to death in the stream bed,
      walled in by a dozen feet of snow.

At this last moment, let essential ice
grip our heart-wood — grapevine, birch,
pine in western mountains.
On their knees on ancient stones,
the gods feed branch after branch,
      twig after twig — pine,
      birch, vine shoots
      into original flames.

      The ashes of our poems
      drift away on an infinite wind.

from

RIP CURRENT

RIP CURRENT

"*Un passage pour l'Egypte se paie en or . . .*"
 — Arthur Rimbaud: letter from Genoa to his
    family, November 17, 1878, five years
    after he had abandoned poetry.

1

out of sea maw
    a frigid wind
    of hurricane force
    late Columbus Day afternoon
    screeches like a fish-eagle
    zooming down for the kill,
    crashes against shore rocks,
    careens into cedars
    spends itself at last
    against vacant mountains
    where its broken wings
    set timber humming
    like a cosmic harp:

(" . . . *a rip current is a killer*
flowing out to sea perpendicular to the shore . . .
suddenly the swimmer discovers he is being swept out
into deep water, waves crashing over his head . . .
almost out of the surf zone
he goes down and drowns . . .")
    a dark wind ploughs the fallow ocean
    into flowerless clods, grassless humps,
    heaved over the salt prairie, finned
    with sharks nosing out of the depths,

Quotations from the *De la Pléiade* edition of the complete poems
and correspondance of Rimbaud. Translations by the author.

death snouts in perpetual motion,
trailing the black raft from the Medusa,
buoyant though freighted with bodies:
can timber be weighed down with any more death?

"wafted by stronger breath,
by faith and devotion,
freed from the wheel of change,
escaping another birth,
forever absolved from sorrow and death."
"A passage for Egypt is paid in gold . . ."

2

Madame stands too straight in the meadow;
her fingers, tightened around her parasol, bleed.
The dust of willows, shaken down by a bird's wing,
still drifts with the river, and remembers . . .

How she hugged every penny, yet spared no expense
to stage the funeral. Stiff-necked upon a parish chair
is she counting the pennies traded for the tapers
in twenty orphans' hands or weighing the silver
melting on the choir's eight tongues,
the gold pouring from the throats of the five principal singers?

Think what she must have spent eight years later
to have his bones exhumed and recoffined
beneath a white marble monument!
"Il durera longtemps," if nothing extraordinary happens.

The brass plate on his coffin still gleams like new,
the grave-diggers astonished everything so well preserved —
the box only blackened a little
by its contact with the earth.

One must be cruel, November to May.
A butterfly hovers over a bank of flowers.
All summer long, haze hangs in those trees
or roves the damp grass like a ghost.
     "Yesterday, a day of great emotion —
     at mass, I caught a glimpse of a young man
     resting his cane against a pillar
     same age, same build, one leg missing . . ."

If a boy gets drunk, it's on the water of the Meuse . . .

3

     "Mon voyage en Abyssinie est terminé."
     — Letter from Cairo, August 23, 1887.

In Abyssinia, the desert is quilled
with trillions of blossoms after the rain.
Time is eternal on the threshold of every tent.
The desert is inhabited by wandering tribes.
There are mountains and a succession of plateaux.
Scrub brush and mimosa swarm with elephants,
all manner of ferocious beasts.

          One yearns for beeswax and honey,
          the pollen of absent flowers
          weighting the thighs of bees . . .

4

          Dear Sister,
          All I want to know is how are things at home.
          Are the crops in?
          Have you picked the apples in the orchard?
          How much did you get for the grain?
          Are the cows still giving milk?

"Send me the best French translation of the Koran.
And buy me a theodolite, barometer, rope, and telescope . . .
and send me the following books:

> *Le parfait Serrurier,*
> *Manuel du Verrier,*
> *Manuel du Fabricant de bougies,*
> *etc. "*

Although there are no locks on the doors,
no glass in the windows,
the beeswax candles burn slowly and softly
at evening in the tents . . .

> "I yearn for the chalky desert of . . ."

5

> *"Vous me choisissez parmi les naufragés . . ."*
> — UNE SAISON EN ENFER

". . . mon existence périclite . . ."
I leave everything to the mountains
and to the rivers.
Only the trees are honest,
and the stones.

> *("A rip current is an insidious ocean action*
> *that can exhaust the strongest swimmer.*
> *Fortunately, the swimmer can tell*
> *when he is in one.")*

Persistent, the bloodstream courses
  secret channels,
replenishing, heartbeat after heartbeat,
  a sea without end.
Spirochetes, like sharks, cruise
after rafts laden with the shipwrecked,
  the living and the dead,
 at the edge of reefs
  beyond unattainable atolls,
zig-zags and terraces which would take an infinite time
  to ascend . . .

The Abyssinian harp burns in my hands
  "I say the strangest things, very softly . . .
 a continual dream . . .
  better to be damned in eternity."
"J'aimais la mer . . . comme si elle dût m laver [me laver de ces
  abérrations] souillures, . . .
  *salut à la bont . . ."**

We call for help. No one hears over the surf's roar.
Panic takes over, then exhaustion.

  Count us all among the drowned.

* From the rough draft of *Une Saison en Enfer.*

MARGINS

*"C'est la mer mêlée
Au soleil."*
— Arthur Rimbaud

1

All afternoon in the spotless sky
Of a dying summer, over the contorted pines
And vacant beach, a sparrow-hawk soars
On banked wings, drawing invisible circles
Across a blank blue page until the margins
Fizzle and crumble under an expiring sun . . .
The margin of error is infinitesimal.
The hawk's talons will grapple its quarry
Before it has a chance to run . . .
    A margin for disaster,
    A margin for luck.
        The sun melts into the sea
        And water and air are one.

2

The Japanese painter,
His brush loaded with ink,
With four quick strokes
Transforms pure white space
Into a dish of plums:
With one stroke the carpenter's plane
Unfurls a perfect scroll —
The board is true to the hairbreadth of an inch:

60

A crime to carve rotten wood! Una gran vergogna!
Blasted Michelangelo, comparing art to love.

3

The light hovers for a moment in the cedars,
The sea's edge grows dim. The light barely moves.
A perpetual drizzle nourishes moss, lichens, ferns.
The light through a screen of leaves
Turns green, then golden
        Along a margin of silence,
         A margin of voices never heard.
A band of fog over sea and sand invades the silver snags.
Crows settle into the cedars as darkness falls:
        A margin of words left unsaid,
        A musical phrase unplayed.

4

On the two-lane highway past the lake
In late afternoon log trucks exceed the speed limit.
The chained logs weep for the raw forest.
Where the river pours into the sea
Salmon sleep, suspended in an endless dream:
        A margin of profit, a margin of loss,
        A symbol for all that does not endure,
        All that does not transcend the perishable:
        A margin beyond which the truth lies
        And the untruth in the uneasy eyes;
        The margin of consciousness, a black river
        Dividing the living from the dead.

5

At night the wolf spider prowls the river rocks.
The ant lion lurks at the mouth of its lair,
Pounces on the ant that crosses its door:

A margin of safety,
A margin to allow for escape.
All summer in the mountains I read the Provençal poets:
"Li dol e·lh plor e·lh marrimen. . . ."
Blind I see again,
Torch lifted against torch under the evergreens:
A margin of hope
Pitted against a margin of despair.

6

Imperceptibly, dust drifts over the still-life
Upon the table, onto the black folds of cloth
In Cézanne's studio at Aix:
fruit, Cupid, long-lost skull,
A margin of life
A margin of death.

On the electric car from Marseilles, the grave-faced farmer
Sits stiff-backed at the edge of his seat,
The brim of his hat dead-level over his eyes,
One of the painter's card players come alive.
He played his cards well.

PHOTOGRAPHS WITH AND
WITHOUT SOUND

*". . . tomorrow we shall be able to look
into the heart of our fellow-man, be
everywhere and yet be alone . . ."*
— Laszlo Moholy-Nagy

1

Edward Weston
I am not asleep
just resting my eyes
and marking time
ein Augenblick
leave me be
you wait so long
for the right moment
to capture what you see
and do not see

2

March weather is
hit and miss
sunlight splatters down
with snow and rain

the creek draining the draw
meanders and dawdles
under matted salal
and huckleberry bush

the wind scours barnboards
until they are off-white
sweeps away old dust
creeps away with a broken spine
to whine under bent grass

frugal Hausfrau
the blackbird whistles
bending a hemlock spire
so easily another inch

that is the way the eye operates
recording what is old in February
and new in March
this year last year the year before

not even the sharpest lens can catch that
one blackbird whistles to another
downstream
a million years ago

3

We see what we do not see:
the invisible made visible
on an April day:
hear and do not hear a small song
in the leafless twigs,
believe and do not believe in the reality
of a white-crowned sparrow
in its scrubby home,
head thrown back in dissonant song —
a sewing-machine-whirr —
preceded by four plaintive notes,
enthralling us as we watch and listen,
showered with dew.

A sickle moon
is nothing but a shadow
mowing insubstantial stalks of light.
The real moon roves out of sight.
A real bird sings a note we cannot hear

until spooked by a dark wind
it darts away.
We backtrack into silence along a winding path.

For a moment "the hygiene of the audible,
the health of the visible"
slowly filter through.

Quotation from Laszlo Moholy-Nagi

EDEN AND BEYOND

Quant' è bella giovinezza . . . the honeyed crown
of your hair . . .
che si fugge tuttavia . . . schist dissolves
on the mountainside.
In the uterine light, pink is webbed with violet.
The wood doves flock after rowan berries.
A fetus stirs in the doe's dark womb.

Between Fiorenza and a flowery American meadow,
between late spring and autumn, your heel
grinds the mountain gentian into dust
beside the high trail. The rhododendron
at the meadow-edge drags a scrawny flower
in the trailside muck . . .
si fugge tuttavia . . .

Between your Tuscan and our Saxon, the full vowels
diminish into flatness, the song of our thrush
fades decrescendo by the stream bed
in the western dusk.
Your blackbird awakens me in early morning,
calling from a window ledge
above the Via Cavour.

The girls used to come down to dance from the hill towns and
dance all night in the market squares of Lucca and Siena,
eyes shining back the early summer moon.
But now the flowers are broken by early snow, dark
couples with dark under the mountainside . . .
che si fugge tuttavia . . .

I move toward love,
toward the muffled shuffle of the dancers' feet.
In a brief review of years,
I fall asleep . . .
che si fugge tuttavia . . .
Send the dancers back to their hills.

Italian from a poem by Lorenzo de' Medici

ON THIS SIDE OF THE MOUNTAINS
WHERE YOU HAVE NEVER BEEN

I remember you otherwise, not so far from home,
your mouth not a black stone,
your hair not a nest of spiders
in this damp orchard invaded by alders
on this side of the mountains where you have never been.

Once in Rome three days before Christmas,
a long time ago, farther from home than you had ever been,
leaning out of the window of a scrubby hotel
on the Piazza di Trevi, you believed the stones
while the opulent fountain dashed cold water on your face.
Two silver coins gleamed on the table
to pay for your passage home.

In the broken bowl of the Colosseum
spilling a cobalt sky out of one end,
you met a woman in a purple cape
who read your fortune in the palm of the arena,
your too brief lifeline drawn in sand and stones.
You gave her a lira for her ticket home.

Now on this orchard floor, patterns of light and shade
come and go and are always the same.
Do our mothers straddling our graves
bring us to birth a second time?

I see you walking where you never walked before,
toward home through the drifting leaves
still smudged with gold, happy, whistling,
your hands in your penniless pockets.

"ONE FEELS A MALADY"

"Banal Sojourn"
    — Wallace Stevens

For a moment at the heart of summer
the ant balances the sun on its antennae,
then lets it drop.

The old malady returns.
Sleepless on separate beds
we spend a banal sojourn like yours in a hypothetical town.
The tubs of hydrangeas still stand
at the foot of the steps.
Their blossoms are fading to the color of ash.
Their dry petals clack like the grackles' beaks.
The sky is no longer streaked with rose.
It is the color of basalt.
All summer, the sow bloated with cabbage, dozes behind the
                                                    privy.

Eyes ablaze, the mongoose
will dodge the cobra's bite.
"The discovery of the double helix
ushers in a golden age," screams the holy idiot.

Infinity, like life, like death, has an appetite for stars.

TARASCON

I want to believe
that the wind from the river
roiling the beds of lavender
in the station yard
will lash out with the same fury
tomorrow and tomorrow

that the woman who sails over
the grimy station floor
on glass feet
her ankle-length gown
molded to the bones and muscles
of her black body
will glide over the floor
tomorrow and tomorrow

now that the snows have melted
in the pastures around Lanslebourg
from the rooftops of Briançon
the wolves no longer slink down
into Paris during the coldest winters

the moon sifts and sifts
the dust of dead poets
from palm to palm

PROVENCE

"There is a sadness about Provence
no one has ever described."
              — Paul Cézanne

The wind god darts from palm frond to palm frond.
The river god stumbles like a drunk
under the bridge.

Only the mountain god retains some measure of composure
and surveys the plain through half-closed eyes.
Esparto grass fractures the flagstones.
Thyme creeps over the thresholds.

We lay our tools aside . . .
polished spade,
industrious rake
jostle each other in a spidery corner.

We count our gains and losses
beside a small fire.

GRAVE AT SÈTE

for Paul Valéry

Beyond the last American ridge, on the cliff edge,
    blue burns to gold at the zenith.
We shade our eyes, glad for eagles;
    count them with one voice.

Before the future year,
    we hold on to their holy circles;

    start from zero:

        the grave under the pines,
        the thud of a falling cone sending
        a tremor through the Italianate tomb —
        the frozen eons of spheres.

        The wasp halting at the entrance of her nest
        is hammered into gold by the sun.

ROME WITH GOLD / 1935

After a thousand huzzas from the fist-lipped sleeves,
A thousand vivas for the balcony's
Bravados, a thousand bravos for the chin that bawls
Its benedictions on a golden age,
And on war, its gold-armed, bald-knuckled saint
Strutting the golden streets in hoodlum boots,

Brides kiss away their golden wedding rings,
And wheat spills golden from redeemed marshes, grapes
Sleep in their golden skins upon gold hills.
Puppets dangle laughter from golden strings
Over the mouths of orphans, gold clocks chime in trains
On time past golden triumphal arches.

The moon burns golden on the walls of ruins
That drift away in clouds of golden dust.
Brides thirst for wine more golden than the grapes
And dream of golden bread they cannot have.

SESTO CALENDE / LAKE MAGGIORE

for Eugenio Montale

I press my face against the train window
hoping to catch a glimpse of the red turtle doves
flocking into Sesto Calende for the first time in anyone's
                                  memory,

while the young doctor, the blue ox yoke he bought in Milan
spanning the luggage rack above his head,
chatters on and on with his two daughters, one dark, one fair.
    The ox yoke will adorn their mantel, he says:
    sky-arch over earth-fire.
    Everything comes to pass.
The mountains at the border melt into each other.
River water melts into lake.

We enter the tunnel under the numb alp,
finally rejoice in Swiss air
between blue wind and gold.
    The fire blinds us all.

74

LAKE QUINAULT

Revolution and revelation amount to the same thing;
tally out to three soft-shelled eggs
squashed by the female's breast
in every golden eagle's nest.

Cold winds scoop up golden air.

A tall owl on the trail stoops to whisper in my ear.
Regal winds wrap the lake in less than regal clouds.
Elk tracks end at the fern edge.

Our car grinds past the last clearcut to the last ridge,
chain saws snarling.

The nature trail winds on and on to terrestrial paradise.
The owl, tall as a fir, blinks at the trail-end.

St. John (Muir), the eagle,
skims the lake on imperial wings.

COAL TOWN

On the roads outside town,
pebble haggles with pebble
over the price of dust,
but dust works all day free of charge,
sprinkling hellebore and youth-on-age.

In town, the wind auctions off
memories of dead miners and whores
in their bituminous beds
to anyone with enough corroded pennies
to pay for them.

All roads leading out of town
climb in switchbacks out of time
up through bull pine
and chunks of granodiorite
to pure air that costs no one anything,
not even the hawks.

Time goes for cheap
on the butcher's block
in the back of the company store.
Eternity hangs from the meat hooks,
the day's best bargain.

SLAV CEMETERIES:
ROSLYN, WASHINGTON

In these cemeteries, a photograph of the
deceased is attached to the headstone.

In six or seven languages, our gravestones proclaim
Our epitaphs to the clouds, boulders, and pines.
Our photographs match our sinuous names.
We laugh at those who try to scan the sibillant lines:

Croation to the wind, Polish to the sun.
How can we persuade the living to believe
That what is done can never be undone
And it is useless for Lena and Binka to grieve

For Mirko who promised them his farm?
Last night we danced in Balkan kitchens, red wine
Staining our lips, with buttery girls, arm in arm,
Our feet stamping out the polka's wheezing design.

A rooster crowed as pure as slivovitz.
The moon dispatched us home, two tottering miles
To our feather beds. While we sleep, the gray cat sits
Upon the windowsill, eyes half-closed, and smiles.

IN THE MINE

Every morning, the ten south windows of my father's house
reproduce ten copies of the sun.
They blaze like ten sunflowers all morning
in the blue plate glass
while my father kneeling in the deepest mine
orders the dark to curl into a ball
that he will place in a corner until he is ready to do
what he had not dared to do before.

Ten minutes before noon, the glass begins to buckle
with the energy of so much light battering its skin.
Balancing the ball of dark upon his palm,
my father holds it to his ear, listens to it hum
fossil music, clear as the voice of extinct leaves
singing on a long-dead tropic wind.

When grosbeaks and waxwings settle on the limbs
of incandescent firs ten seconds before noon,
the ten windows shatter, scattering blue splinters onto the
                                    ground.
In the mine my father hurls the ball against a wall,
stoops to gather the pieces and fit them together again.

FEDERICO

In Granada, a long time ago,
I wanted to take the bus to Fuentevaqueros,
visit the house where you were born,
its red-tiled roof swarming with mourning doves,

but did not go. Franco was dying
in Madrid. The Guardia's stubby fingers itched,
hugging black leather holsters all through Spain,
and I never walked down your street,
never saw the cows coming home from the pastures
and drinking the icy water from the Sierra Nevada
at the trough by the village fountain.

Instead, I contented myself with the Alhambra
and the nightingales grieving all afternoon
in the elms in the long ravine,
and was baptized three times by holy gypsy hands
immersing me in the black waters of *cante jondo.*

A year later in Geneva,
I watched a black rat scurrying from corner to corner
of an excavation as the workmen beat
it to death with picks and shovels.

UNDERSTAND THIS

Understand this:
I live animal days.
Evenings my eyes grow heavy with trees and sky.
I turn over stones, hunting salamanders.
It is warm close to your blood.

You are the dark your roots make.
We converse in extinct languages.
You are neither woman nor ghost.
I have forgotten your name.

You are an hour of water.
I pour you into sand.
You are a ship without sails, beached on the rocks.
Your eyes shine in the dark. Your pelt smells like rain.

Slowly I evolve into a lemur.
I covet branches, hang from them
All day by my thumbs
While wolverine and rat bring another day to ruin.

You are the shade on a wall.
You are an hour of thunder, an hour of rain.
Your nakedness is tanned by African blood.
You prepare your eyelids for a dangerous dance.

I balance you like a hawk upon my wrist.
See: an abyss begins at your hairline!
See: you are a crater into which I pour the dark contents of
                                        this pitcher!

See: you . . .

Based on a poem by Gottfried Benn

80

PHAEDRA

Nestled among the five hills of my palm, a leathery sphere,
A snake egg, pure as a stone beside a mountain tarn,
Imparts dry warmth to my skin, and I think I feel
A distant heartbeat echoing my own.
The birth tooth on the snake's blunt snout will rip it free
To glide across the gravel to the shore,
Enter the icy water, battered into gold by the sun.

In Paris, the summer heat blasts the black façades,
Bleeds down blue dust from the prowling stars,
While the racket of traffic on the boulevards
Tumbles our sleepless bodies against the walls,
And marble bulwarks brake the serpentine descent
Of the Seine. Suddenly, the river coils, uncoils,
Tenses for a strike, spilling the black barges
From its scaly hide.

Or we imagine an endless sea behind a classic stage,
Hear invisible waves scrape the edge of boards,
And see or do not see toward the play's end
The water buckle, reptilian, cold — advance, retreat,
Advance again, crash down upon us in our seats.

I lay the snake egg back in its darkening nest.

LA QUAL NULL'ALTRO

"La qual null'altro allegra arbor nè fiore . . ."
— Giacomo Leopardi, "La Ginestra"

You insist, your shadow pinned to the ground,
on being strong
where you find your homeland and birthplace.

Last night a vicious wind off the ocean
banged the dry stalk of the clematis
for hours against the side of the back porch
until only the roots remained.

In Seattle, by the clear lake
sprinkled with fallen leaves,
in sight of the icy backbone
of the fierce mountain,

Sterminator,
white destroyer
threatening us with magma and mud,
the wind rushed between us,
snatching your words away.
I knew they were important,
perhaps even fatal,
reading your lips.

We imagined
pumice, ashes, stones,
ground out of the thunder-shaken uterus of the
mountain,
raining down upon us.

Entering the house in the dark,
we slid the deadbolt home.

. . . But your frail stock is immortal
framed by fate and your own hands.

BEADS

I'll not take back what once I gave: the dark kiss
from my golden mask's silver lips,
but will take back again what you will never miss —
the crimson garment that clung so tightly to your hips,

and leave you the frame on which it hung,
clean and empty but very beautiful
like a useless string on which red beads were strung
by fingers that were especially careful

not to spill them on the floor
to be gathered by sons and daughters on their knees
and be locked unstrung in a box for

ever and ever and ever. Imagine a hive of bees
surviving all winter on honey the color of the sun
until the combs are sipped clean, one by one.

LADY, THE WIND

Lady, the wind will find you, and the water
And earth and fire, where you dance,
A whirling figure on an island's earth
And its flowers. Transfigured by the ocean's song
Into a watery creature, you arrive at birth
A second time and are acknowledged
By the birds and fish as the one
They waited for so long, and born
Again you cannot ever die.

The spider recognizes you, and the ant
Believes your dance upon the rocks he owns.
Do not forget that a woman's dancing soul
Can take the shape of some bird or animal,
The raven or the beetle or the mole,
And inhabit some dark loathsome place
And haunt the dreams of all the island's crones.
The light that pours across the ground
Is all the light that fell across your face.

The mineral that feeds the rose root's hunger,
The seed that nourishes the bird
Have fed you too. Your father's anger
Had made you pale. Two births promised a third.
This island, its light and trees and water
Surround you where you dance, your thighs and ankles,
White in the shadows of the summer leaves.
The mouse watches you; the owl ready to pounce
Upon it knows your name. Only your father grieves.

The ocean does not grieve, nor does the earth.
All things not human love your face.
Long ago you sang another death
Upon your olive-branching island. Soul
And soul embrace and sing with one long breath,
Remembering your face, summer's daughter,
But light can never make you whole again.
The earth will have you and the water.

MOVIE HERO

I swagger past the ladies and tip my hat.
I cry hey to the scaffold
and hi to the rope,
and my heart aches.
My body spins in a phony wind

before the false fronts of the movie set
under a black mountain and a cold cloud.
Gunless, a rider gallops past my gallows.
Riderless, a mule trots past my grave

under the gold nugget of the gambling sun,
the flipped silver coin of the loser moon.

TROLL

I limp out of the world's end,
a bag of fish bones on my back.

Like a troll reeling out of the earth's
diamond gut, I sneer.

What thick-footed bear stamps
out dance rhythms in my ankle bones?

EARTHQUAKE

Self-righteous winds preach to us,
Harangue us from the summits of four hills.
Which wind huffs from farther away?
Four winds intimidate the stars.

The old man nods to us from his chair
Upon the front porch, leans back and guffaws toward the door.
The winds stop preaching. The moon steps down
From her ladder and scratches the windowpane.

I suppose only the crows know what is going to happen.
They crowd each other off every branch.
We can hear them cawing five miles away.
Then the ground begins to shake

Like our old dog shaking the rain from his hide.
And the winds begin preaching again
From four directions, and the stars all flap away
With the crows and settle down with them in the boughs.

The old man is asleep.

CHRISTMAS CARNIVAL

The moon mimics the sun. Blue apples weigh
Down boughs, spent coals of summer, sapless fruit
For starving birds. Pale root is entangled in root
In the iron ground. But the air still smells like hay.

The stars bed slowly down. Our friends pitch a tent
For a cold Christmas carnival in the wood
Among the weeds trampled into oozy mud
By Iceland ponies and an African elephant.

The dog-lipped boy begins to howl. The hippogriff
Is dumb in three dead tongues. God Jul! Joyeux Noël!
Brown-skinned girls scream upon the carousel.
The queen is crossing the pond on a skiff.
The children kiss her hands beside the canvas walls
And ride away with her upon her animals.

EARTH TAILOR

I sew the way the roots go,
Take my orders from a stone,
Bargain only with the mole and the worm.
Stitch on stitch with a needle of bone,

Crafty as a spider spitting threads,
Leaf on leaf, I ply my trade,
Cross-legged under the ground,
Tailoring rags of shade,

Blind and tongueless, horny thumbed,
Warp crossgrained to woof, humus to must,
I deal out my fabric, yard after yard,
Half autumn compost, half winter dust.

THE TOWER OF SILENCE

I

We lay our dead, naked, on the tops of towers
To be picked clean by the birds
Gliding in on the wind, reptilian,
Hawk-beaked, harpy-winged,
Ripping out heart and lungs,
Sea and sand blazing as one in the sun.

A procession, blue on the seaside,
Led by a hag in a cowl,
Circles the cape at the seamark.
Gulls and their shadows haunt the stones.
The horizon blurs in a haze of silver and white.
The wind answers the bird-voiced bones.

The doors in the tower are all shut tight.

II

He came from a death's distance away
Through intenser silence than he had ever known.
        Not even Procris lying on the shore
        Surrounded by herons and indifferent dogs
        Created more silence in the way she lay.

And then he summoned music from the strings,
Plucked a wilder lyre than he had on earth,
        Strummed song out of chaos,
        A beginning of form

Growing out of the light that followed him
To where she stood among the rocks
        Faltering toward his song.
All the nightingales of Greece,
Made wild, sang in the serpentine dark.

O the dead are young forever and ever.

III

The earth is his poem: the sun, his metaphor.
Fire sings like a bird on the stone.

Having broken the sacred circle, murdered
The she-snake coupling with her male
At the marsh edge among the yellow mallows,
A goddess' anger upon him,
He was turned from man into woman,
Fluent in the language of birds,
The kingfisher's, the crow's, the heron's,
The jargon of the wren.

IV

The laurel tree is for change —
        but only into death.
He wrapped his arms around its trunk
in front of the grotto
        by the beached sand,

an old man, ivy-wreathed,
drunk, wearing a tattered dress,
a string of bells jangling around his waist,
        blind, shrieking in falsetto,
        frightening the doves
        in the sacred trees,
        so they flew away and back again,
happy Grossmutter
muttering incantations to the wind.

Lady of Dark Places,
  take him by the hand,
  guide him over the rocks
  and around the slippery logs
  at the river mouth.
Do not let him fall.
Open a pathway before him.

    V

A branch in the hand is an eye,
The seasoned wood of cornel,
A staff in the hand of the blind
To see the way along the seapath,
The rocky road to the ships,
The beaked ships of the warriors.

A bird for the blind is a voice
That speaks the country's language,
The measured words of wisdom,
The level call of truth
On the dusty seapath
By the beaked ships of the warriors.

The sun on the sea is a flame
Kindling the charred sails
And broken oars of an autumn voyage,
Propped against the splintering keels
Of the beaked ships of the warriors.

SURVIVAL

I shiver through a winter
but survive.

Swaddled in blankets,
I huddle over the stove,
count every stick I feed into the fire,
coax embers to blaze again,
ever so briefly.

All week a wind from the East
has pounded tenpenny nails of ice
into the cabin walls.
The thermometer by the door
has zoomed down past zero.

My frozen breath hovers over my head
like the ghost of the last dead poet
I have read.

Asleep, I wake to sleep again.
Sleepwalker, I track down polar metaphors
across the frozen floor,
awaken with the cold brass doorknob in my hand.

Asleep again, I dream
of a single leaf,
that rasped for days by the wind,
still clung to the alder limb
beside the creek until it finally fell.
Now sealed in ice at the creek edge,
it too will survive the winter.

from

DOG STAR

DOG STAR

Dog Star and dog fox stalk the dying year to its end.
Fox flame, star flame flare for an instant
In the year's last hour.
Fox tracks, star tracks trail away across the snow.
Heart fire, hearth fire flicker on a bed of stones,
Portents of what will go, what will remain:
Embers flaked with ash.

EMBERS

That the smoke of autumn's smouldering leaves
is yesterday's history,
and the ash that remains, tomorrow's memory
is obvious enough.
Who needs more explanation than that?

Embers smoulder in the spinal cord,
sometimes bursting into flame:
a passion to live life over again
when you thought it was forever dead.
Who remembers in what direction the smoke was aimed
before it veered off on an opposite wind?

100

LILACS

The lilacs are in full bloom
In every corner of the overgrown yard.
I smell them everywhere.
The spaces between their blossoms and leaves
Are blue caves, swirling with dust.
Roofs and cupolas of a foreign city
Seem to float out of the haze.

But in the nursing home next door,
The air conditioner announces the first warning:
By autumn, the necropolis will be full.
There will be no more room for the living,
Not to speak of the dead, in the mausoleum.

But there will still be time for love
After so many loveless nights,
A time to get drunk on wine
After so many months of thirst.

THE NORTHERNMOST ISLAND

Ice-cold rain mixed with hail,
Dog grass beaten down,
Wind sharp, honed like a blade,
A sick moon posing as a sun.

Frost has welded earth-clods iron-hard,
Turned turf tufts black as embers.
The sky will always favor ice over rain.
The advantage is all December's.

A wild goat lurches as a barnacle goose,
Cut adrift from long-flown flock,
Whirrs off honking at his feet.
Hoof-horn skids on rimed rock.

The old Irish poet is long since dead.
The pony is no longer tethered to a post.
The dog's barking is at an end.
The new moon rises from the old.
Ghost clings to ghost
In a tremendous wind.

TIME

Time, the mongrel bitch,
limps along on three legs
up and down both sides of the street,
sniffing each bush and clump of grass,
every garbage can overflowing
with a whole week's waste.

She holds a bleeding forepaw
tight against her chest
and whimpers from time to time.

Not long ago on a greasy pallet
in a basement,
she whelped a dozen pups
sired by Pity, a hopeless hound,
toothless and blind.

Piebald and wall-eyed,
all of them have succumbed
to accident or disease.

In heat again, trailed
by a troop of panting mutts,
she is ready for another round
of births and deaths.

THE MOTHERS

Faust: *Die Mütter! Mütter!* . . .
     —Joh. Wolfgang von Goethe, FAUST II

"Le noche delle Madri s'inaspriscono, cercano il vuoto."
     — Eugenio Montale, "Nel Parco di Caserta"

Silver endures, and tungsten, in the sinuous veins.
Bronze leaves, welded into wreaths,
Shine, perennial in windless air on the black vault.

     But the yolk curdles in its shell.
     The egg is long overripe.
     The cormorant sits in vain on her nest at the cliff's edge.

The Mothers are cruel.
Their knuckles knead stones.
They covet ores, metals beyond rust,
Ageless, dustless.
Their fingers tighten around gold for keeps.
They crave mountains of bronze.

FOR SPAIN

1975

I

Through your most distant landscapes,
what news of you? What guitar twang

in the half-light at dusk among the stone houses,
on the alley cobbles littered with goat turds and straw,

on our way to the gypsy caves,
night's first dark seeping like stains across our faces?

At home, fox fire illuminates the stumps
in the thickets at the swamp's edge

while our thrush, not your nightingale,
fills the cedar trees with absolute melody.

Both birds elaborate the same theme
all afternoon, not love, not death,

but birth in the crotch of a branch,
the clutch of eggs hatching under the female's breast.

Suddenly song dissolves into silence.
The light hardens into stone.

Only the topmost leaves sing on
in archaic Spanish or long-dead Arabic.

The dark follows. Snails shed
their shells. Stones lean into dust.

II

The main thing is freedom, said Paul Klee.
The freedom of the imagination, he meant:

the spirit free at last of the body's weight.
But do we always have to be looking for the dead?

Still let us give the dead poets their due:
Góngora, Calderón, Lorca, all who sang

in the half light at dusk or the full light of noon.
It is said that the hotel guests covered their ears

with pillows when they heard shots ring out
at midnight in the cemetery on the hill.

Crossing the border, the Moroccans are locked in a room,
told to stay there until the next train leaves

at nine in the morning for Algeciras and the ferry home.
The generalissimo is dying in his oaken bed.

In oilcloth hats and pasteboard boots,
patrols glide along the greasy streets

in twos. The morning train stops at a village,
nameless, cool water gurgling in irrigation ditches

beside the tracks, dividing meadow from meadow,
a small bird's voice bubbling in the leafy dark

of the elms along the road, invisible,
insistent that it be heard, even by a trainload of strangers

entering Spain . . . *oh rossinyol en flama!*
In the cleft between two hills at home

a stream trickles on through salal and fern.
Swainson's thrush sings all afternoon.

III

At the periphery of your landscapes
at the sea's edge, brine eats away the artifacts,

the little that remains of the long dead. We are more at ease
with them than we are with the living.

Let us pay homage to all of Spain's tongues, living or dead,
from mountain and vineyard, arroyo and waterless plain,

rimed or unrimed by all of her poets!
The seafloor is strewn with lost relics.

The dark is everywhere. It follows
the moon into the lemon trees and the olives.

Between the third planet and the ninth,
the hunchbacked moon and the limping stars

sing in an extinct language. The birds respond.
The blue whale has almost vanished.

Where will the tigers go? Who killed
the dusky sea sparrow's mother?

How long ago did his father sing in the reeds?
We read a poem in a language we do not understand,

look up all the words in a dictionary.
The lines break in two and hang like a broken web

strung by a long-dead spider in the dark,
from branch to branch. The broken web sways under our
                                                            breaths.

IV

All for Spain:
>and every Spaniard who ever sang
>greetings in a spirit of grace,
>>hello, goodbye,
>>>and hello again . . .

Have confidence in the dust.
Trust the water.
The dead sing through closed mouths.
Everything was not said in the beginning.
Nor will it all be said in the end.
The stones cry their bird cries in the night.
The sea breathes in.
The sea breathes out again,
>And all the beach is bones.

THE GRAPH

The dead osprey in the sand,
the coyote rotting under the silver log
by the river mouth:

There are various ways to contemplate
the evening in the vicinity of death.

The wind blows from the south, then the north.
Four crows squawk in four dead trees.

> *Dost thou make wide thy fields?*
> Alcuin's epitaph
> purifies the page
> on which it is written
> like a wordless graph.

The hunter goes home.
There is no other place.

THE FIRES OF LENT

Now I understand
the strength of trees
digging nourishment
out of stone with ease.

Through the leafless orchard
the long-legged runners race,
knee-deep in darkness,
torch light staining hands and face.

They fling hissing brands
into apple branch and pear.
Wheels of fire spin
through breathless air.

Leaping like cats
they scatter sparks like rain,
toss their torches
higher and higher again,

wave their fire-pronged branches
— hacked from pine —
around leaf and tendril
of the ailing vine,

brandish their pure tongues of fire
across bark and knot,
exorcise leaf-curl and scab,
rust and bitter rot.

MARSTON-BIGOT, SOMERSET

New Year's Eve, 1945.
1262 Engineer Combat Battalion,
billeted on the grounds of the former
country house of the Earls of Cork.

Some crazy bastard from Company A
sets off a couple of real road busters
precisely at midnight on New Year's Eve
in the orchard below the chapel and manor house
of the ninth Earl of Cork,
blasting the old year out, the new year in,
frightening off the owls from apple tree, pear, and plum,
rocking the earls in their graves in the churchyard,
setting the tower bells jangling a ghostly change,
rattling the German glass window in its frame.

Somewhere a wall falls, and another,
and a last year's hornet's nest
drops from the eaves to the ground.

The stage properties belonging
to the Admiral's Company — 1570 —
overflow the world's bins:
there is no more room in the world
for all the world's junk:

1 rock, 1 cage, 1 tomb, 1 Hell mouth;
1 tomb of Dido;
1 glove, & 1 golden sceptre;
and the city of Rome . . .
1 golden fleece; the cloth of the Sun & the Moon;
2 coffins; 1 dragon in Faustus;
1 wheel & frame in the Siege of London;
1 crown with the sun . . .

A long ways off a long time ago,
Mole shuffles across the carpet in threadbare slippers,

proposes a toast, as soon as Rat and Badger are seated,
      to the fire on the hearth,
      the fire in their hearts.

MORELS

In mid-May
among the first trilliums,
under the pines and white firs,
the first morels,
feigning fir cones,
push up through humus and duff.

We fill a basket,
sauté a panful in butter,
smack our lips over the taste of earth.

KONTRAPUNKT

I crave another body.
This one will never do.
I have had enough of these arms.
I envy a bird's wings.

I no longer want these fingers.
I crave another body.
This one will never do.
I think of the river's hands
shifting pebbles from palm to palm.

I cannot see the wind nor hear the light.
I crave another body.
This one will never do.
The goshawk's eyes
can always locate the right wind
to soar in: her ears can hear the light
speeding past her.

I crave another body.
This one will never do.

SHADES OF GRAY NEAR BRUSSELS

Black laid beside white
dissolves into gray.

"I am writing you
from this backwater in the hills
straddled with barbed wire . . ."

A rooster and six blue geese
practice close order drill in a red brick courtyard.

A man with a scythe
slashes at a bed of red poppies.

Blood-red petals litter the walkway,
plaster themselves to our heels.

The figs of Carthage are plumper than Rome's.
The senators get the message,
rub new salt into old wounds.

We shall never be rich.
No use hoping for prosperity.

Still, there is no money in being patient . . .

EARLY AUTUMN DARK

Slowly at ease, at home among the firs,
A horned owl milks the early autumn dark
Upon the ridge side, hoots a hollow note
Timed to the pulse beat of the climbing stars.

I turn and turn upon my frost-rimmed bed,
Drift off to sleep to wade through slopes of snow
And skate my way across a sheet of ice
Above the timberline, the owl hooting below.

Grappling a sheer rock face, rotten, cold,
I hang in panic over nothingness.
I scale a glacier into darkening clouds
On bare feet. I pray my toes will hold.

But slipping, I plunge into a blue crevasse,
Lie stunned, face down on frozen rocks.
A mile away beneath the timberline,
The owl still hoots, braiding a rope of notes

As strong as hemp. Loop on loop
He deals it down to me in my dark dream.
Hand over freezing hand, knee jostling knee,
I climb out of my nightmare on his voice.

THE NIGHT A CHUNK OF THE MOON . . .

How could we forget
the night a chunk of the moon
plunked into the lake,
sending tons of water splashing
over hawkweed and dandelions,
and thousands of starlings splattering
like dust after an explosion
into the air?

The stones cried out in pain
on the roadbed.
They couldn't move.
Blind milestones wept for a hundred miles.
One mile was as long as a thousand
for the fleeing ants and snails.
One minute was as long as a century
for the dying butterflies.

What light was left in the chunk
that fell that night from the moon
drained away into the lower valley
flooding it to the brim
with the palest light
we had ever seen.

COTTON CANDY

The night before the Fourth of July
The Big J Carnival pulled into town.
And on the Fourth the lot was prettier than Christmas,
But I'll take the Fourth over Christmas anytime.
And Come on, Daddy, buy the kiddies some cotton candy,
And Hey, Lady, win yourself a real-life kewpie doll!

Big Lou, the Man with the Iron Lungs, ate fire like a fiend,
And Señor Manuel, eight feet tall,
Swallowed two swords at once.
Somebody shot the Tattooed Lady in the belly with a bean,
And the crowd roared.

But nothing beat the Snake Lady from Brazil
When she grabbed the baby from Joey's wife
And kissed it on the forehead
As the rockets went off in the stars.

KNIVES

Poems should be
like the knives
my dad used to make
out of old crosscut saws
and car springs,
blue-bladed,
honed to razor sharpness
that could shave the hair off his arm.
They would bend but not break,
their handles carved
out of walrus tusk or walnut,
northern, tough,
perfectly balanced,
fitting the palm,
great for skinning rabbits,
slicing meat from the bone
for the hungry belly.

AT LAST

At last I am the old survivor
I always wanted to be,
lingering late in my garden,
scraping the ashes from my shoes.
Humpbacked, I walk with a limp.
Half-blind and deaf, I read the lips of the dead.
I can say hello in nine languages
and good-bye in twenty more.
Old friends are used to what I say.
All winter, I have nothing to do
but set hopeless traps for wolves.
My wife knits mittens
for the village children.
Crows come and go
in the cottonwoods by the river.
The hour hand is missing from our clock.
Sometimes the minute hand goes wild,
sweeping time before it
so fast the clock dances on the table.
My wife and I dance with it,
around and around
all night until the sun
spills through the windows
and lifts us off our feet
and carries us away
like a flood.

ABSENCES

*

She stands barefoot in the wet grass
beside the house, looking in the window,
her pale face reflected in the black glass;
ivory duplicated in horn,
caught up in a double dream:
a true one and a false.

*

The light of North America not far from the ocean
in mid-winter is the light in the spaces between the spaces,
the light between the light and the light,
the light that is there and the light that is not.

*

My mother walking home along the railway track
from company town to company town,
past the coal bunker, along the filthy creek,
her crippled son wrapped in a shawl in her arms,
met a woman weeping beside the track,
but the woman vanished like the ghost of a deer
into the woods when my mother came near.

*

Yellow as a many-petaled dahlia
in my mother's garden, the sun spins
over the abandoned mine,
the miners buried under the sandstone seams,
the mules' skeletons under the corral,
the tipple long gone,
the wash house and the powder house,
holes in the black ground.

Timor mortis conturbat me.

GO TO THE WINDOW

Go to the window:
tell the dead crowding the street
not to stand there but to move on.
Tell them when I fell from the ladder
and broke my neck
I didn't die.
Tell them I don't want to join them
in their civil war of the dead against the dead
or in their futile battles with the living.
Tell them I am not one of them.
Tell them the door is locked
and I have lost the key.
Tell them the telephone is ringing
and someone wants to talk to me.
Tell them a policeman is waiting to arrest me.
Tell them my wife is leaving me,
the baby is crying and wants to be fed.
Tell them I am not dead.
Tell them anything so they will go away.
Tell them to go home to bed.

THE GOLDEN MASK

An image burned where no light ever shone
Behind the eyelids of a man born blind.
Deceiver of mortality, his dreaming mind
Led Death among the measures of a dance in stone.

What if the golden mask around his face
Is all the skin his skull will ever wear?
There was no earthly fire could sear
That flesh begotten in an earthly place.

Can marble hold him, dust and ghost,
Or darkness keep him safe in stone
Until the golden mask crumble on crumbling bone
That wore a face transfigured by the light it lost?

THE PATHWAY

The river meanders where mountains cannot go.
I skirt a field where doves take wing.
Overhead, the power wires sing and sing.
Upon the lakeside, the wind breathes slow.

The shadow of a silver snag floats in the lake.
I gulp ice water to slake my thirst.
Three hawks hunt, loose-winged over trees, immersed
In the slack light their circling makes.

I choose a pathway into black trees.
The hawks still drag the light they made.
The wind tracks me down into cold shade
Through maidenhair fern and anemones
And grapples at the roots of my hair.
The pathway drops off into empty air.

A SECOND EARTH: *PRESENCES*

1

We pace back and forth on the shrinking floorboards
all morning, all evening long,
like your prisoner in that city so far north,
more "concerned with living than understanding."
All summer, all autumn,
the sea comes in, the sea goes out.

Finally, it is winter.
Salt bites into the crusted earth.
Black trees shine over their reflections
in the black ice on the asphalt pavements.
Chickadees tilt tail feathers
into the wind.

Christmas comes at year's end
with holly nailed to the warped door.
*"I have to save my own skin,
and that is my greatest concern,"*
scribbles Kokoshka in his diary.

And that is our greatest concern.
A new ice age inches southward.
We nurse the fire, keep moving,
not out of boredom but to save our skins.

2

Black Mountain, Cold Mountain:
we catch a glimpse of mallards
flying low through fog,
aiming for the East Fork of the Quinault.
Elk tracks vanish at road edge.
An old man crouches in weeds
in a haze of flies and his own stench.
Black geese shoot northward over ploughed fields.
Swans whistle in nearby pastures
between highway and river, rock and rock.

Colonel Chivington's Colorado Volunteers shot
pregnant Indian women, cut out their pudenda
and stretched them like raincaps over their saddlehorns.
White Antelope, Black Kettle,
sing death, sing death in the broken grasses.
Sing death, sing death.

The last grizzly was killed at Corral Meadows in California
in 1922, all of them disappearing from Oregon in 1933,
one still roaming the Skookum in Washington, not far from
                                        Hex Mountain,
or so someone said ten years ago.

We try to remember the red tree mouse gone forever,
killed off by clearcuts and slash burns.
It spent its life in the tops of firs and hemlocks,
never touching the ground,
scurrying among the stars in the moonlight,
drinking dew.

Colonel Chivington's Volunteers
were trained to kill Indians:
Cheyennes, Arapahoes, Utes.

The mouths of the dead are stuffed with grass.

White Antelope sings:
   "Nothing lives long.
   Only the mountains and the earth last."

3

The cat stalks the shrew through sheep grass.
We come to the river, wait to be ferried across
to the mud village on the other side.
The road will continue through bare brown hills
at 12,000 feet, the passes at 17,000, to Shigatse.
We can scarcely breathe.

A woman in a long black skirt,
bright apron around her waist,
stoops over a field under a black mountain.
Her hoe is heavy.
The gods are weary.
They smile through heavy lidded eyes
from the mountain top, watch her work.

Incense of burning juniper branches
blows out on wind.
We pass a power station humming
with the energy of a hundred-thousand gods.
Om chimes from the walls
and *mani padme hum*

Stones take a long time to grind barley.
They grind it very fine.

4

The darkness in the tunnel delays the day-dreaming traveler
for a moment sitting in his chair beside the fire.
Like the loon steering toward her nest in the reeds,
the moon floats toward the leaves, rides high in the branches,
and we are aware of the first stars before we see them
tangled in the higher branches of the yellow pine
beside the cabin door, and we breathe in deeply,
inhaling more light than air.

The Milky Way streams from branch to branch
like thick cream poured by the hand of a god
at a scarred table in an old man's room.
Fruit bends the branches of the tree of life.
Overripe peaches thud to the ground
for the golden deer in the golden grass.
The saffron cougar hunts on the mountainside.

5

One summer morning, the pheasant whirrs
out of the long grass beside the path . . .

How shall we track the spoor of love around the world,
the dark smudge of radiation at the heart's core?
Should we try a Geiger counter? It will not work.
Or consult Nietzsche or Marx?
What do they know about love?
Patience, mom âme, et courage. Pazienza repeated
the squint-eyed crone in Italian to my father
as she stood by the gate, cursing in Venetian, then Tuscan.
She had to be a witch to be able to curse in both.
When I reached out to help her over a root
in that green Italian wood, I felt nothing but air.

Witches were common in Apulia and Lucania
before Horace's time and Ovid's, long before Rome.
Naked gods danced in the sunlight
beside gurgling streams pouring out of slits in the
                                        mountainsides
where the entrance to the underworld was hidden by brush.

Amber light beyond the imagination filled the woods
when my father, Gioann Sergent, was born in Canavèis,
"doussa terra" as Peire Vidal called it,
so many of the Provençal poets struck by the beauty
of the *"tozas"* from the foothill villages: Casellas, Sanh Jortz.

Faeder, Pare,
deliver us from our memories.

     6

On our hands and knees in the intricate tangle
of fir branches and twigs,
we grubbed out the hard buttons of Boleti
pushing through dirt, white nuggets in our palms.
Sliced, stewed in their own juice, until they are golden,
they lie on our plates beside the golden cake
of corn meal, polenta for the native gods
of the North American woods and mountains
in another light, on a second earth.

"Le bele tote." Bertran de Born would have understood
such mountain talk from high peaks and saw-toothed ranges,
jargon from the mouths of miners in the Golden West:
"ël përtus," an orifice and more:
a gate into Paradise, our shoulders brushing the golden pillars
as we hurry into the garden, lush with Italian fruit.
In a bower of beauty, her skin is real.
Loving her, the perfume of orange blossoms and honey,
the scent of dust, are enough to make us faint.

Rust devoured the front-yard gate long ago.
The lilac trees are long dead.
The mountain river races down the valley as cold as ice.
I wash my hands in its water and dry them in the sun.

LE VOYAGE

"O cerveaux enfantins!"
— Charles Baudelaire, "Le Voyage"

1

For the two boys fascinated by maps
and *The National Geographic,*
oh the happiness of going somewhere,
the planet shrunken to a ball on yesterday's page,
yet how immense in the pool of light under the lamp!

Getting up in the first light
to a thousand white Leghorn roosters
crowing in everybody's backyard,
to the wailing whistles of the black locomotives
straining uphill to Stampede Tunnel
with a mile-long string of freight cars
clanking behind them,
we shiver in our BVD's, blind fingers
hunting buttons and slipping them home.

We leave, heads wreathed in flames,
ride off to the pumping rhythm of the pistons
of our old black '23 Chev
down the gravel road that winds on forever,
past fenced fields and pastures,
the meadowlark dribbling
flute notes across the dripping grass;
we lift our faces to the wind,
drunk on blue space and light,
the sky blazing overhead;
sail past islands of pine glades
floating in lakes of lupine in bloom,

so much blueness around us,
so much more heaped ahead,

blossoms so dense under the pine trees,
pillars crumbling and falling,
the weight of Venice,
lighter than goosedown,
yet too heavy for its golden roofs,
walls and stalls giving away to the awful tonnage
of so much blue air, the golden horses
charging across the blue lagoon.

II

. . . heartweed scattered along the roadside,
 heart leaf, heart root,
 heart scald, heart grief,
 heart's-ease for the lovelorn,
 heart-whole for lovers,
 heart balm for the sleepless,
 heart break, heart ache
 for what has never been,
 for the unseen, the unheard
 beyond Lost Lake on the way to Quartz Mountain;
 the trail along Fortune Creek
 climbing to the watershed
 dividing East from West,
 dark from light, day from night:
 heart wish for the Heart Father,
 heart beating in time with heart.

III

Up the valley, a curtain of haze
hugs the mountains' roots, hangs in the hollows.
Mid-morning, the sun will burn it off,
begin to glare in our eyes
forcing us to look at the ground.

133

But at three in the morning the air is still cool.
Shadows flank the mountainsides,
lie like pools under the trees.

Love counts what counts:
the distance between light and shade,
the distance between the road and bed,
the distance we still have to travel . . .

    IV

    Bindweed clambers over the roadside rubble,
    the detritus of last year and the year before,
    binding us to time and weeds.

    High over our heads, pine boughs
    nurse their secretive blossoms.
        Father Anthers,
        Mother Stigmas,
    can you tell us how far we are from home?

    We fall asleep beside our father, wakeful at the wheel.
    Clouds of pollen shower the old black Chev
    in the moonlight under the stars,

        gold piled upon gold.

NOTATIONS

1

I have been blind from birth
and now suddenly see
the fields of bunched grasses,
the black birds of prey.

2

A black wind blasts away the ark.
Where have all the birds and animals gone?

3

At last I am a handful of dirt and seeds,
a ground-up stone, a black gem.

4

A tree is what the seed intends,
where darkness ends and light begins.

5

A river is not here for a moment,
pouring noisily over blue gravel.

NEW POEMS

1997

THE POET AND THE VOID

In a letter of June 27, 1884
Stéphane Mallarmé responds to
Leo d'Orfer's request to define poetry.
— *Selected Letters of Stéphane Mallarmé*
        edited and translated by Rosemary Lloyd

1

You pack a wicked punch! Blinded, I reel.
You ask me to unveil the secrets
Of poetry and how it sings,
Zero in on all its mysteries,
Explain away its magic properties . . .

Bruised, I stammer . . .

I refer you to that melancholy bird, the heron,
Anchored on one reedy leg,
The other tucked beneath her breast
Beside an unruffled lake,
Hypnotized by her mirrored image,
Oblivious to the silver scales, the metal flashes
Of minnow mouthfuls at the water's edge . . .

It's her own reflection she spears and not the fish . . .

2

Or I remind you of another dream,
The swamp lily hooded like a cobra in a bog,
Illuminating with its inner light
Its outer self: spathe and stippled bloom,
The tragic beacon of an ordinary life . . .

139

3

Imagine, if you can, pure emptiness,
The Void where Word and what it names dissolve
In the mind of a god weighed down with the world's grief,
Contemplating Nothingness, head clasped in hands,
Seated crosslegged on the grass,
Crowned by the light of an absent moon.

CIRCUS

"My circus animals were all on show . . ."
— W.B. Yeats, "The Circus Animals' Desertion"

Where have your animals all gone:
Shuffling ape and elephant?
A great wind whips the circus tent,
Rips the canvas top from end to end.
Poles bend and groan but do not break.
Guys strain. The taut ropes sing like birds.

"O Love that sings the calm heart's naked song
That in the dark flesh rings, frost-clear and strong."

Two voices and then a third sing out old words
To new-found notes. Dark drum, darker guitar
Support the melody, repeat the soft beat of the heart.
The north sky crackles with electric light:
The great aurora of the longest night.
A lost bird cries. Star collides with star.

READING*

We came to hear you read and be our guide
Through our own dark and pathless woods
And walk with us a while beneath high trees
By quiet waters, warblers as thick as leaves
Singing full-throated in the summer shade.

A few had come to watch you bare your soul,
Another few to hear you thump the drum
Of poetry, strike up a rum-tum-tum
Upon a hide stretched taut across a barrel
To entertain and titillate
A cheering crowd packed in a circus tent.
What did they take you for?
A carnival barker or old clothesmonger?

Instead, you danced, did fancy toe-steps —
Your friends, the bears, dancing at your side —
Until you danced yourself into a thirst that you could bear
                                                    no longer.

Raising the water pitcher to your lips
You drank straight out of it.

It's deeper water you would drink.

*At this reading Theodore Roethke read his magnificent poems, often
accompanying their rhythms with the inimitable dance steps he sometimes
performed in class. Toward the end of the reading, unable to bear his thirst
any longer, he raised the water pitcher, which had been placed near the
lectern, to his lips and drank directly from it.

THEY KNEW WHAT TRUTH IS

Someday someone is bound
to translate the stunted spruce trees
at the tundra's edge by the black water and ice
      into Truth.

And someone will order the kestrel and kite
to gorge themselves on Love and leave
the lemmings and voles alone.

Let them direct the dirt
to be kind to César Vallejo
and Cesare Pavese, to Celan, and Trakl,
all the poets who were hurt or hurt themselves.

They knew what Truth is, and Love. They understood.

THE BADGER

The badger and the shrike
deserve your respect
for what they are,
for what they are not:
the hooked beak,
the claws that strike.

The night before the battle, Caesar on his cot
had a nightmare and screamed in his sleep.
What the sword has conquered the sword cannot keep.
The wise men and the simple have given that all their thought.

The enemy upon the treeless plain
is picked off one by one.
A battle is lost.
A battle is won.

The badger and the shrike
deserve your respect
for what they are,
for what they are not.

SKY BURIAL

Lhasa 1988

The sky buries
what the mountains cannot
and the kites and ravens have spared:

chunks of flesh hacked clean from the bones,
chucked helter-skelter across the rocks
for fox and shrike to finish off.

Few of the late dead will ever attain enlightenment,
find everlasting peace,
be free forever from the wheel of craving and pain.

At the threshold of the monastery door,
we step over mastiff and mongrel cur
sprawled across the dusty stones:

herdsman, king . . .

CROW

The winter left him craving summer's weather:
The blue and golden light of trees and stones
Upon the cold hills that he thought he saw.
A man's dream was of water and of wings,
A warmer landscape brighter than the snow
Comforting his skin beneath the winter sun.

He imagined a greener country, all canals and meadows,
While birds on every branch on every tree
Believed him, singing winter was a lie
Of old bones craving a nearer sun.
What had that crow cawed on the frozen river?
"Our eyes see what they want to see. A crow
Is still a crow in winter or in summer."

The crow is right. So were the Chinese poets
Whose crows are always crows, not symbols of a soul,
Those drunk old men who really knew
A winter's weather cannot be a summer's,
And though the soul will sing in harmony
With all the instruments: oboe, flute, and violin,
Until the voice of each is but the voice of one,
The voice of each is still its own.

I GO BACK

I go back to my old scars,
wince at the long-buried pain,
taste my wounds on my tongue.

I cry out to you with my uneasy bones,
knitted into an aging frame
crowned by a hawk-nosed head.

How can I free myself from this shifting light
that turns birds into trees,
trees into birds, rocks into what they are not?

Let the wren burble away in the laburnum.
A blurred animal crouches in a seed.
Expect another birth soon.

THE NAMES OF GRASSES

Dog-tail Grass
Purple Fountain Grass,
Cloud Grass,
Little Quaking Grass,
Brome,
Hare's Tail Grass,
Canary Grass,
Hawkweed,
Campion,
Wall Barley,
Cock's Foot Grass,
Soul's Grass . . .

Grasses . . .
Named and nameless,
Grasses that are grasses only in name,
Wild grasses and tame.
Mothers of yeast and bread,
Old ferments in the earth,
Keepers of secrets . . .
Grasses rooted so they cannot move,
But only reach toward the light.
Air moves in the light,
Light moves in the air.

The old oak chair
Stands in the room, covered with a wolfskin,
Hide and hair,
Throne for a poet who is not there.

"Warry, shift . . ." *

* Walt Whiltman's last words, his instructions to Warren Fritzinger,
  his nurse, to place him in a more comfortable position on his bed.

WIND AND BIRD

The wind in the cedars is pure.
It sings and sings. I stand where I can hear

A woodthrush on a bough, repetitive singer
Of only one tune, slow but sure.

He says what he means and what he means is true.
I watch the shy bird zigzag away through ferns.

     *

I stand where I can hear the wind and the bird.
The wind is still. The bird has not returned.

Between the light of the dying sun
In late afternoon and the light of the moon

Rising with the stars, what is that voice I hear?
The voice of another bird or the voice of a different wind?

COYOTES

We are fascinated by the photo
in an old *Life* (or *Death*) magazine
of eight dead coyotes strung head-down
by their hind legs from a barbed wire fence,
their muzzles and front legs cinched tight with wire,
as they dry to board-like hardness in the wind,
their bellies slit open down the middle for their
bladders to bait fresh traps for the rest of their kin.
The sheepherder who set the traps jogs along in his 1950
                                         pick-up
to Boulder for a couple of beers.

The dehydrated carcasses of the coyotes
swing and clack in the wind like castanets . . .

A hunting hawk over the fenceline barely breathes.
Only the stones breathe more slowly.

IN HIS HOUSE OF WOOD

A man kneeling on stones to light a fire,
Hands cupped around a match and its flame,
Could rise and surprise a god or ghost
At his shoulder and never ask his name

But welcome him to his house of wood
And offer him bread and wine
And find it strange but good,
More ordinary than divine,

To talk to him, listen to his tales,
Before the last flame dies
And never learn his name
Or care whether he tells the truth or lies.

TREE

You are all the light you make:
leaf, branch, and bole:
Darkness pours from your crown to your roots.
You are perfect and whole

like a stone or a hawk,
a rare kind of gold.
The nights have grown longer.
Day and night are so cold.

What will the young men do
in the light they have left?
The girls will tie on their sashes,
place right foot next to left,

and begin to dance, and dance
through the lightless night.
The young men will dance with them,
place left foot next to right.

MORE TREES

Hölderlin's Pears

It is not easy to disregard
  The death of trees:
  The long-rooted blossomers
Toppled by saw or disease —

Great trunk, tender stem,
  Leaf and broken bough
  Consigned to flames,
Laurel, chestnut, hemlock, and haw —

Fruit trees, apple and pear,
  Loaded boughs that will not break
But only bend, reflected
  In a flawless lake:

The endurance of a passion
  That allows the branch to bend
  And not to break
In a day and night that never end.

WHAT THE SEA SAYS

. . . between the sea's audible voice and its inaudible voice
the moment when the osprey's screech carries the farthest
echoing from the cedars on the nearby rocks
the moment when one does not hear what the sea says
only the too loquacious gulls debating the crows
by the tongue-tied cliffs

there are moments like moments on a lake
cruised by snow geese more beautiful than swans

between what the sea says and does not say
between its ominous soothsaying and its silence deep
as night the vacant spaces among the spruce tree's branches
between white wind and green-blue wind from the east
sanderlings scurrying up and down the beach
in a black mist
we open the window our fingers interlaced on the sill
like the sea's fingers entwined with the land's
we are two trees joined yet separate
stranded at the dark's farthest edge . . .

clanging of the sea's clapper against the night's bell
a buoy astray on the full sea
long ago signaling danger torn sail splintered keel
a clutch of crab pots raked into a tangle of sea grass
kelp verbena running insane over black sand
sulphur polypores transformed into hardwood
on the trunk of a dying fir
Kore ploughing deep furrows on sea on land
the sea's fields the land's

there are other moments in clapboard houses
detritus of clocks and clock parts dead wood

154

heartwood punk wood plant and blossom pine planks
warped wearers of weathers dead roses plastic flowers
blown off a grave snagged on the wire strands of a fence
broken green bottle by the road

    Eugenio's chestnuts exploding on the hearth
love's fire the heart's health wine on the table
on a remote planet not ours wasp nest smouldering under
the eaves in torrid summer sun
dark woven into dark at the flame's edge petal
upon petal stigma stamen golden anther of love's rarer roses
pressesd with crumbling leaves in rain-warped books debris
wreckage flotsam rubbish rubble junk
useless paraphernalia reeking under the wheeling stars
morning planet and evening star father and
mother of old habits fathers of fat mothers of mold take us
by the hand stop your chatter lead us to the table
crammed high with feasts . . .
                  We hear birds singing . . .

SEKHMET

Lioness-headed,
        you stalk dangerous game —
        that wild animal, Love —
        across the desert,
        elusive and wary.
Springing out of ambush,
        you grapple nothingness,
        snap your jaws at empty air.

CAMPANIA

Bless the grain.
Bless the black grapes,
the green oil in the jars.

Another winter wheels away with the stars.
Ice gloats that its turn has come again.
Naked trees shiver away their shapes.

Then summer continues its wars,
the brutal sun its raids on the ripening grapes.
Dust lusts for rain.

But summer's loss is autumn's gain.
Rising Venus escapes
the arms of Mars.

Bless autumn's grain.
Bless the bleeding grapes,
the bread on the table, the oil in the jars.

LICHEN

Stone-splitter, granite-cruncher.
   rock-gripper, grinder of dust,
    strange duo of two appetites
     churning away as one,
    manna for famished tribes,
      savior   waster
your own hunger is boundless and your strength,
      creator   destroyer
           Shiva
               and
                    Shiva again . . .

OCTOBER

October breaks every branch
over every stone.
The wind, half-beserk, mauls
the cringing woods.
What can stand upon the earth,
leafless, moon-ridden,
under such crazy stars?

WE COUNT HOURS

HAMM: *All that loveliness!*
     — Samuel Beckett, ENDGAME

We count hours
from zero to zero:
listen to the termites
digesting the old timbers
of our house.

At sunset, we climb
to the high window over the harbor,
watch the herring fleet sail over the horizon
toward the docks, decks heaped high
with squirming silver
in the light of the rising moon.

The women come out of their houses,
with wine and bread for the famished men.

THE POET

The roses you pricked your thumb on
in your garden at the end of summer
have come to life and are blooming again . . .

THE PATRIOTS' FLOWERS

A mè fieul, Màrio, mòrt sël Génévry

On the summit of Génévry
on those wild crags,
on the battle ground
where the fighting raged for ten days,
now that the summer sun
has returned to scorch the stones,
as weightless as feathers,
smooth and colorless as down,
the first Edelweiss flowers
are blooming again.

But this year, if you break off a flower,
you will notice with astonishment
it is tinged
with an already fading half-shade of dark rose
as if a thread of blood,
running from leaf to leaf,
were winding through the plant from deep within.

The currents of morning air
from the woods above
cry out to the pine trees
rooted on those wild crags
and whitened mounds of stone
that the patriots' flowers
are the color of blood.

Translated from the Piedmontese of Nino Costa, whose son,
Mario, an Italian partisan, was killed on Mount Génévry in
the Alps on August 2, 1944 by the Nazi-Fascists.

THE OLD CAT

A True Story

Seven chipmunk tails,
one for each day of the week,
are laid out, lined
in a straight row on the arm of the sofa
by Olive's old cat
after he has gnawed them off
and feasted the bodies and all,
the wicked beast.

The Major's old scimitar hangs askew on the wall
The rickety house shifts on its blocks of stone.
The happy cat dozes on the sidewalk in the sun.
The west wind meets the east wind in the trees.

How long has Patches, the old cat, been dead?

STONES

Late August swells to actual green
Bestowing reluctant opulence
On common ground. Plain stones
Nestling among commingled grasses
Beside a mountain lake
Are rare jewels. Transported south
And laid among emerald reeds
That bull frogs boom into,
They would be foreign to that place.

Munificence of wilder green,
Superfluous with hotter light
Would only smudge their luster.
No stone could shine at its best
In air so affluent with reckless vines.

Such stones belong
To higher elevations
Beside a mountain lake
Like eggs of some antediluvian beast
Heaped upon the shore.

BOY SHOOTING AT BLUE
GLASS BOTTLES ON A STUMP

All afternoon he plinks away at blue glass bottles
on a stump, scattering blue splinters in the grass,
careless of what the snake said to the ground,
or what the roots meant to tell the pines.

The sky was almost too pure,
burnt to gold around the edges.
The hawk and the forked branch were one
above the slough too far for a gun.

Between two crows squabbling in the pines,
And Venus rising, there was a long way to go.
Between the canyon floor and a cloud, the bottles
whistled back the wind. The bullets flew.

Weeds swayed and bent in four different winds.
The hawk on its branch cocked his eye at nothing at all.
Who could remember the pictures nobody painted?
The poems nobody ever wrote?

All afternoon, he plinks away at blue glass bottles
on a stump, scattering blue glass splinters in the grass,
careless of what the snake said to the ground,
or what the roots meant to tell the pines.

GO TO THE DESERT!
FIND THE LION'S BONES!

1

Warty-thumbed, I plant leeks in my starving garden,
row after row, for the fair weather to find:
papery onions, redundant chives.
I drop to my knees on the spongy loam,
pray to the god of garlic to save the world.

2

I call to the owl
on its way from Eden to Hell.
Be my friend!
Be my friend until eternity comes to an end!

3

We dream in a field of mullein.
Mountains close us in on every side.
Invisible frontiers separate the ant hills.
There is always the same sleet, the same rain, the same snow.
Nothing ever changes, not even the wind.

4

Tell that red-tailed hawk to save my eyes.
I have a hard time distinguishing the shades of wind,
telling one kind of light from another,
hugging the mountains, not letting go.

I did not know there are so many colors of dust.

5

Rocks are scattered about
for the wind to count.
It counts them one by one,
multiplies by zero,
divides by one,
subtracts what has been lost
from what has been gained —
a day's profit, a night's dreams.

6

I read lips, spell out words and dreams,
interpret your eyes, decipher your skin.
I study languages all night, living and dead,
and spend hours trying to break the heart's codes.

A leaf is hard to read.
A stone never speaks.
Corners lisp in the dark.
The stars sputter.

Often they are mute.

I listen for clues,
some rumor from the wind,
what goes on on the moon.

7

What languages do the leaves speak?
How do they say "stay" or "go"?
How do they translate "love"?

They rarely want to speak,
and when they do, they speak so fast
I cannot understand.

8

What has been bought?
What sold?
Did the thistle sell its soul?
Who tried to buy the sun?
Auction off the wind?

Is everything for sale?
The heron's feathers?
The paws of the mole?
The light of the waxing moon?

In time, we lose count of the number of sales.
There are too many to count.
Too much to charge to the air and the dirt.
Too many grains of pollen
in the cells in the bees' hive.
Too many grassblades on a grave.
Too many footprints of a mouse
leading across a windowsill,

If everything is for sale,
what can we lose?
If we can't pay cash,
we will put it on hold.

item pd to god
item pd to ij divells

item pd to wormes of conscience
item pd to iiij angels

9

Keeper of bees, pay attention to your hives!
Protect them from the winter winds,
        the autumn rains!

$10 paid for smoker for bees
$20 paid for a hive of bees
$20 paid for gloves
$1 paid for veil and hat

10

Go to the desert! Find the lion's bones
    the jackals have dragged across the stones.
    Feast on golden honey from the combs
    hanging in the rib cage,
    dripping in the skull!

The lion has given the bees a home.

"What is sweeter than wild honey?
Stronger than the lion?"

    Whiter than a lion's bones?

THIS IS WHERE THE SNAKE DIED

I

None of summer's undulations
        of wings and winds
or all of autumn's transparencies
        of leaf or air

can make you more beautiful.

II

Her face is a leaf from another garden
beyond weather, beyond the fiction of other seasons.

III

I stalk a bird into its song.

IV

I would translate seeds into words
. . . if I could read them.

V

The mountains sleep where not even the moon
can find them.

VI

The wind blew all night,
pushing the dark away from the sea
and turning the river black.

VII

This is where the snake died
and was born again from his skin
in the only valley I knew.
My skin walked into the sun
without my bones.
I knocked twice upon a door,
ivory or gold,
and said I was lost.
Which way was home?
I could only guess where I was.
My bones were ignorant
at the edge of the hay field
under the trees where the mowers slept.
My hair preferred to hide in the shadows
where I waited for a girl, Hebrew or Greek,
with a voice like a myth.

I could not see or hear.
The wind got in my eyes.
The light roared in my ears.

WHAT THE HAWK NEVER KNEW

Finality is not what the plover thinks
Nor is it the dream of two merging streams
Becoming one. Only the hawk can tell us
If and when there is an end, but he will not say.

At the zenith of mid-July,
Dogged by an angry star,
I could listen to you murmuring forever,
Leaf-tongued over the creek's bed in the soothing shade.
Maybe I will.

I have nothing else to do.

I TALK TO STONES

I talk to stones beneath deep streams
And ask them what I want to know.

The day is fast, the night is slow.
What dark shades haunt an old man's dreams?

The eagle drives away the crow.
The sun has set: its light still gleams.

Nothing is ever what it seems.
The moon is fast, the stars are slow.

A solar wind begins to blow.
Around, around the sun it screams.

So now, where will an old man go
To find his way, search out new themes?

The ivy climbs, the nettles grow.
What dark destroys, the light redeems.

AFTERWORD

For some four decades now Harold Enrico has been publishing poetry, and in the opinion of many, his is one of the strongest voices in contemporary North America. Enrico has a remarkable ability to blend the imagery of his own Pacific Northwest into the traditional line of the great Europeans. With images that reverberate in the reader's mind, his poetry strips away the nonessential, creating a richness of impression seemingly at odds with his pared-down language. He is a poet who writes of everyday experiences in everyday language, and yet his ability to penetrate to the essential gives him a bardic, visionary quality that leads one to speak of his poetry in terms of myth. Indeed, the title of this "Selected and New" — *A Second Earth* — with its Dantean associations of the new life, its Platonic echo of the world beyond shadows, and its recognition of the environmental movement, points to the possibility of presence and presences.

At the moment, Enrico's poetic reputation is somewhat difficult to determine. At various times in his long career he has been recognized as an authentic voice by the likes of Theodore Roethke and George Woodcock. His poetry has been included in prestigious magazines such as *Poetry (Chicago)* and *Botteghe Oscure*. Similarly, it has been praised by *Choice* magazine. Yet for all the applause, Enrico is still not widely read in his native country. Indeed, he may well be better known in Canada, in part because his books have been published by Canadian publishers. In the 1960s when he submitted poems to *Prism international*, a magazine published by the University of British Columbia, they were immediately accepted by the editor, J. Michael Yates. When Yates later founded Sono Nis Press, he published Enrico's first two books, *Now, a Thousand Years from Now* (1975) and *Rip Current* (1986). In 1990, this tradition of Canadian publishing was continued when Cacanadadada Press published *Dog Star,* Enrico's third book. Indeed, Enrico has come up to Canada often from his home in Washington State to give readings. And now once again it is a Canadian Press that is publishing his selected poems.

The classic quality of Enrico's poetry is immediately apparent in its tonalities. When George Woodcock first came across Enrico's poems in the collection *Dog Star,* he was immediately struck by their superb rhythms and the assurance of the language. As a critic well-read in the European masters, Woodcock was also impressed by Enrico's participation in a poetic tradition that stretched back through contemporaries to the French symbolists, the Italian Renaissance, and further back to the myth-creators of Greece, Egypt and India.

That Enrico should be so fully immersed in such a tradition may come as a surprise when one discovers that he was born in 1921 in the little coal mining town of Cle Elum in the central Cascades of Washington State. Enrico reminds us, however, that these coal mining towns in the mountains of the Pacific Northwest comprised a veritable united nations. Enrico's father had emigrated to the United States from the Canavese region in Piedmont in northern Italy. His mother was born in the Graian Alps, not far from the French border, and grew up in the frontier mining towns in Idaho and Washington State. Enrico recalls how he spent his youth in the Cascades among peoples who spoke many languages. In fact he grew up hearing as much Croatian, Polish, Piedmontese, Venetian and Lithuanian as English. Moreover, in the early twentieth century the people of this coal-mining region often moved freely across the international border, looking for work in both countries. Consequently Enrico grew up, not parochially, but feeling himself to be a citizen of the world, yet at the same time, as a member of the Italian minority, needing to become American. When he began writing poetry at age fourteen (with various languages in his head), it was natural for him to want to write in a world tradition, in which the present was created from the pasts of many different peoples, many different nations.

Thus it was that when he went off to the University of Washington, he studied music and French literature. World War II interrupted his education, and he saw active service with the U.S. Army, 1262 Engineer Combat Battalion. It was during this period in the army that, like so many Americans, he made his first trip to Europe — France, Belgium and Germany. After the war he returned to the University of Washington to complete his M.A. in the French department with a thesis on Arthur Rimbaud and Hart Crane. Shortly after, he won a year's scholarship to the University of Pavia, Italy, at the Collegio Borromeo, where he studied the work of Salvatore Quasimodo. When he returned to the United States, some of his translations of Quasimodo appeared in *The Nation*. He received his Ph.D. in Comparative Literature from the University of Washington in 1970, with a dissertation on Giuseppe Ungaretti. Thereafter he was on faculty in various colleges — mainly Grays Harbor College in Aberdeen, Washington — where he taught foreign languages, humanities, and English. During these years he also returned to Europe most summers to keep up his languages and to stay abreast of the latest trends in writing. In 1985 he retired from teaching.

Helen Vendler, whose essays on poetry for *The New York Review of Books* have been enormously influential, commented recently that, for her, one of the tests of great contemporary poetry is that one should hear in it echoes of earlier poetry, so as to be aware that the poet is writing within and to a poetic tradition. As has been indicated, this is certainly true of Enrico's poetry. The critic for *Choice* magazine remarked that "Enrico pays homage to artistic community with a mastery that is always contemporary." Frequently, Enrico takes for his inspiration an earlier poem or phrase, and one finds that many of his poems include epigraphs from writers such as Lorenzo de' Medici, Rimbaud, Whitman, Lorca, Mallarme, Hölderlin and Benn. At times he even offers translations or imitations of these poets.

It is worth pressing Vendler and others on their reasons for finding it so important to write within the tradition, since, for many today, the tradition is dead. The answer for poets such as Enrico is that his own insights recreate and reinforce those of earlier major figures. As Northrop Frye has maintained, all poets contribute to the unfolding of a single grand narrative. Enrico acknowledges his debt to earlier poets for the language, the symbols, that are his inheritance and that allow him to write from his own experience. He affirms the richness of the moment even as he records simultaneously the approaching darkness and dissolution. As well, language itself — the language of the now, which is also the language of the past — is essential to bring that paradox into relief.

For all his involvement in the European tradition, Enrico is also a profoundly American poet. American history and landscape have fascinated him, and he has taken as one of his major projects the forging of an identity that includes both his present-day experience in the Pacific Northwest and his heritage as a European. His ambitious poem sequence "The Fleece of the Ram" develops from a multi-levelled awareness of exploration as subject matter. The title refers to the Argonauts in search of the golden fleece, but the poem sequence begins in a literal search for America that includes excerpts from the logs of the early Lewis and Clark expedition to the west. Just as the poem's development mirrors the search for America, so it recreates Enrico's search for his own self. As a young boy he was fascinated by the Native American Indians who still picked huckleberries in the mountains and sold them from horseback in the town, and he often played at being an Indian. In the poem, he introduces this desire to be an Indian alongside the historic struggle by the Yakima Indians of his area in the 1920s to maintain their identity.

Thus the poem in its development recreates the literal western movement within America along with the psychological process of individuation, fully conflicted, which arose from the creation of present day America, with a supposedly inclusive spirit that in fact excluded many. One senses the struggle to fit in, to find a way to be both American and Italian (not even Italian, but Piedmontese) — something new. To do this, Enrico found it necessary to move outside American popular culture to find a sense of being that would account for his own growing sense of the complexity of America. As he says: "Cesare Pavese, Death had your eyes, / not the eyes of an American starlet, / blue, blank." The end of the poem also signals the end of the search, for here Enrico makes a voyage in his dreams to the point where he is wide awake, sinking his "fists into the fleece of the ram." The golden fleece has been won, victory is his, it would seem, although the victory occurs only in dream, only in poetry. The poem's complexity was already suggested in the poem's epigraph — an explication of the Chinese character MEI: "beautiful, a big sheep; also abbreviation for Ya-*mei*-li-cha, America." The present volume includes the Chinese character itself, something that was lacking in the earlier edition. At the poem's end, the poet, like the Argonauts, has captured the golden ram, which is also beauty and America. That the poet creates this union of opposites in dream, in poetry, and not in life, indicates his recognition of the distance between poetry and life, a recognition that reveals Enrico is not prepared to follow the many romantics who imagined poetry's resolutions to be also the resolutions of lived experience.

What Enrico aims at in his conjoining of the European tradition with the American landscape is a way of seeing that recognizes and affirms the paradox that light shines forth from darkness. In his early poem "From the Top of Quartz Mountain on the Twenty-fifth Anniversary of Kandinsky's Death," Enrico begins with a perspective from one of the local mountains, which allows him to reflect that "deer, trees, the shapes of stones" are the emblems of "Great Perfection." That they arise from the heart of the Mountain suggests an older, almost

Aristotelian sense of an *anima* at work in the creation of the world, an *anima* that expresses the different patternings of *things*.

The development of this concept of living pattern occurs in the next section, which seems at first almost an aside (it is set off in parentheses), when Enrico is reminded of Kandinsky at Neuilly as he "mixes his own colors" and waits for the precise moment to let the light into his studio to be expressed in his paintings. The nature of the *anima* or form that Enrico finds in Kandinsky's art reverberates in the natural world at his own doorstep in the Cascades. For Kandinsky "in the center of each painting, / zero is absolute in a timeless zone," while on Quartz Mountain the sun explodes into "black begetting black at the edge of red." There is nothing here, one notices, of a benevolent deity or a providential natural law. Rather Enrico ends with the stanza: "Yama, how your blackness shines, / a black bird in a nest of stars!" One of Enrico's early critics guessed that Yama must be a Native American spirit. But in fact Enrico has gone much further afield: in Sanskrit, Yama is the Lord of Death. Unlike conventional wisdom which has goodness and life as positive, here Enrico invokes blackness that shines, "a black bird in a nest of stars." That black becomes white, that black shines into white, reveals the paradox that our awareness of death also creates our awareness of life, that the one is necessary for the other. They are not separate but conjoined — a concept that goes back to early mythic thinking, one that lies at the heart of the tradition to which Enrico acknowledges his debt.

At times, Enrico's identification with the flora and fauna of the Pacific Northwest becomes so intense that his poetry suggests he is no longer *apart from* that world, but a part of it. In this regard, his poetry bears similarities to other poets writing at about the same time. One thinks of the early poetry of Susan Musgrave written while living in Haida Gwaii (formerly called the Queen Charlotte islands) or of Margaret Atwood in her Susanna Moodie poems. In a poem like "Grizzly," Enrico creates a sense of himself immersed in a world of factuality that permits him to become the wild bear that he pursues in his dreams. Indeed, by the end of the poem he has become so much at one with the world of things that the "sweet smell of the beast clung to my hair / and penetrated my skin." Eventually he becomes the bear itself:

> Furred, my hands stretched their claws
> and scratched at the early stars . . .
> In a nest of leaves
> I slept the winter out.

Here the dream state, the imaginative act of creating the poem, leaves him "furred," protected "in a nest of leaves," where he can survive — both literally and figuratively — the long winter.

There are few poems from Enrico's war experience, but one that stands out is "Marston-Bigot, Somerset" in which his recollection of a soldier's setting off a series of blasts to celebrate New Year's eve, 1945, causes him to reflect on how history fills up the world with "junk" from the past, junk that perhaps needs to be blown away. One is reminded of Pound and his ironic line in *Hugh Selwyn Mauberley* about fighting the war "For two gross of broken statues, / For a few thousand battered books." Enrico's poem shows him only too aware of how the past and its traditions can become a burden, can actually crowd out fresh, vital experience. Indeed, for someone who pays such attention to tradition, it is with a knowing irony that he lists the stage props of the "Admiral's Company," a famous acting company from Shakespeare's time. The props — including "1 tomb of Dido" and "1 dragon in Faustus" — enabled the stage company to recreate every part and character from the past. But as Enrico recognizes, they are also "junk" that crowds out the living. Faced with this sense of accumulating "pastness," Enrico does not invoke any grandiloquent poetic principles. Instead, he brings onto his own stage some of the most domestic characters ever to be created — Mole, Rat and Badger from *The Wind in the Willows* — the very essence of everyday life in the home. In his "threadbare slippers," Mole proposes a toast "to the fire on the hearth, / the fire in their hearts." It is a fine moment in which the comforts of everyday life, exemplified by the "fire on the hearth," are juxtaposed with the life impulse itself — the "fire in their hearts" — which keeps them going in the face of a world becoming ever more burdened by the past.

Enrico has never been one to celebrate war and its supposed victories. As he says in "The Badger," another poem that draws on animals to make a moral point: "What the sword has conquered the sword cannot keep. / The wise men and the simple have given that all their thought." And yet as Enrico knows well, such sententiousness cannot be the whole of poetry. Thus to ground the thought in the things of this world, he concludes the poem with a return to the animal world:

> The badger and the shrike
> deserve your respect
> for what they are,
> for what they are not.

This ending encourages us to see the world, not only in terms of what the badger and the shrike are, but what they are not — indicating that they are to be valued in themselves, not for what they can tell us about ourselves.

Enrico's links to the poetic tradition also allow him to escape the Enlightenment perspective (still very much present today) that sees the world as a collocation of objects to be studied and categorized. When Enrico returns again and again to the natural world, it is not just to find what Eliot would have called the objective correlative for human feeling, but to show how humans and their feelings are in fact part of the natural world. The very notion of the "objective correlative" implies that the human is separated from the natural in a way that has much to do with Descartes' separation of thought and feeling, humans from other animals. But for Enrico, humans grow out of the natural world, and their feelings, their thoughts, are part of that world. Enrico works through the Enlightenment objectivist view to that of a world cohesive with meaning. In a poem entitled "More Trees," which might suggest merely an additive principle, Enrico draws on Hölderlin and his observation of pears being reflected in water, to gesture towards "The endurance of a passion / That allows the branch to bend / And not to break / In a day and night that never end." For Enrico, the tiny plants of the world, such as in the poem "The Lichen" are seen as embodying the contradictory impulses of the universe. The lichen is "stone-splitter, granite-cruncher," but also "manna for famished tribes," and in its contradictories can be seen as Shiva — creator and destroyer.

That Enrico is still writing poems at age seventy-six is a testament to his continuing belief in the importance of poetry. He says that the poems come more slowly now, but they still come. Certainly the section of "New Poems" reveals Enrico still at the height of his powers. "Boy Shooting at Blue Glass Bottles on a Stump" describes a young boy plinking at bottles on a stump, completely unaware of the world around. One is reminded somewhat of Wallace Stevens and his jar in Tennessee, but Enrico captures the beauty and intensity of the natural world from which the boy with his purposeful but meaningless action is cut off. Since there is no one to record the "other" moment, one has a sense of that moment lost, for "the hawk on its branch cocked his eye at nothing at all. / Who could remember the pictures nobody painted?" The reply, of course, is that the poet himself has painted the picture for us. But as Enrico whimsically implies, the picture centres on the boy with the gun. There is another picture to be painted, that we need to become aware of. The poem itself calls our attention to it, to a story of "what the snake said to the ground," but which we have still not heard. In such ways does poetry express that which can be implied only obliquely.

While obliquity may sometimes be necessary, the new poems are also noteworthy for the clarity of their language. As Enrico has grown older, his language has grown simpler. The final poem of the collection begins, "I talk to stones beneath deep streams," surely the incantation of a shaman. One is reminded that for all Enrico's involvement with the European tradition, he has not neglected that of the Natives of North America, and indeed the two traditions may have similar origins. As he says, "Nothing is ever what it seems." The task of the poet-seer is to lead us below the surface, not necessarily to some absolute, but the recognition that "What dark destroys, the light redeems." One hopes that Harold Enrico will be granted many years still for the writing of such luminous poems of redemption.

Ronald B. Hatch
University of British Columbia